20 Feet Deep

How the Sermon on the Mount Kept Me from Drowning

Dr. Dan R. Stewart

Twenty Feet Deep: How the Sermon on the Mount Kept Me from Drowning

First Printing: 2015
ISBN (Print) 978-1-48358-004-3 (Ebook) 978-1-48358-005-0

To purchase additional copies of this book, please contact Dr. Stewart at dstewart@ lifepacific.edu.

CONTENTS

This book is dedicated to my wife, Connie, who has endured reading through my writings and listening to my teachings, and encouraging me all along. I would also like to thank the congregations and students who have heard these lessons over the years and agree that in applying them, there is great reward.

Introduction

This book is based on the tradition, according to the book of Genesis, that the flood waters rose twenty feet above the highest mountain. Therefore, a mere twenty feet marked the loss of all life. The ark was the means by which humanity was saved. God saved Noah, the animals, and his family from drowning because of Noah's obedience in listening to and applying God's Word.

The Sermon on the Mount gives us eight swimming and boating lessons that Jesus teaches to keep us from drowning. The eight Beatitudes, when inverted, form a workable outline for the rest of the message. The persecuted and the poor in spirit become the bookends, with the first and last Beatitudes proclaiming the kingdom of heaven as a reward.

Close consideration is given here to the natural divisions where Jesus declares, "You have heard that it was said," and how the subjects He addressed change; as such, the Beatitudes, in an inverted order, form the title and subject for each of the capsulated teachings in this book.

When we realize that drowning is evitable, the teachings of Jesus become the lifeline to keep us on top of the water, or in the boat with Him. These eight lessons are to be applied and practiced like a child who needs to know how to become "water safe". The Christian needs to practice these lessons to become "spiritually safe." Though none of us will ever be able to swim long enough, or construct boats great enough to keep from sinking without Christ, these lessons show us how to apply the teachings in order to keep from drowning.

This book uses textual research in observing, interpreting, and applying Scripture, especially as found in Jesus' Sermon on the Mount. It is not an exegetical work, employing historical and critical methodologies. Instead it is a work of practical theology, which emphasizes the scholarship of application, teaching, and preaching.

My Journey Toward God

My journey toward God began well over thirty years ago. This beginning was less a casual introduction than a radical transformation. My parents made sure we went to church when I was a child and certainly lived as godly examples. However, like many teenagers, I formed a path through willful disobedience, which led to many wrong conclusions.

At the age of seventeen, I was arrested for drug possession, which had been an on-again, off-again affair. Though the arrest occurred early in my life—and though God had clearly used it to speak to me—I would not experience God in a way that shook my foundations (or at least my world view) until my late teens, while I was selling Levis one day in a clothing store.

As I read in our local newspaper that day at work about the account where all the passengers had died in a recent horrific plane crash, I heard God clearly speak to me in an audible voice, although no one was around. He posed this simple question to me about where I was heading in my life: *"If you had been on that plane, where would you be right now?"*

Until that moment, I had not given much thought to my demise. My answer to God's question was quick, and a single word seemed appropriate—lost. At the time I was not in a church, and no one was witnessing to me about heaven or hell. It was simply a cognitive answer to a very real question. God was drawing me to Him. Like a river wearing down solid rock, God was cutting through the walls I had so carefully constructed in my life.

I started attending a church close to our home and found a peace there unlike anything I had ever experienced. It may sound cliché, but the truth was, I was changing. The friends I had spent so much time with began to fall away, distancing themselves from their now "religious" friend. I wish I could say my experience was instantaneous, but it was more like a process through which my road began to narrow.

Some of Jesus' concluding remarks in the Sermon on the Mount are, *"Enter through the narrow gate. For wide is the gate and broad is the road that leads to destruction, and many enter through it. But small is the gate and narrow the road that leads to life, and only a few find it"* (Matthew 7:13-14).

My road seemed like a full-blown freeway—then, lane-by-lane, caution signs began to appear, declaring that the road was under construction. New friends, great Bible studies, and a trip to East Africa transformed my mind, my heart, and my life—transformed me into a disciple of Jesus Christ.

When I began to study the Bible, I was directed by mentors to start with Matthew. The Sermon on the Mount and specifically the Beatitudes became my life verses—my swimming lessons in the sea of life. This message served as the basis for the lessons that helped prevent me from drowning and got me heading in the right direction. I began to read and memorize the sermon and made personal applications, as they seemed fit.

Though I failed often in my application, two passages in the sermon encouraged me to keep striving. Matthew 5:19 states, *"Anyone who breaks one of the least of these commandments and teaches others to do the same will be called least in the kingdom of heaven, but whoever practices and teaches these commands will be called great in the kingdom of heaven."* Then there is the bold declaration in Matthew 7:24 that says that *"everyone who hears these words of mine and puts them into practice is like a wise man who built his house on the rock."*

I personally believe that the Sermon on the Mount is more about endeavoring to be like Christ, than about presenting an impossible effort, because without Christ, no one could live by these standards. But, as we were made to be like Him, these teachings have become a way to know whether we are living with His blessing.

I was drowning and this message gave me lessons and guidance about how to swim when impossible storms come—or sail when my boat is taking on water—with no fear of drowning.

Over the years, I have read many commentaries and books in which the authors give a plethora of interpretations for the Sermon on the Mount. One of the best overviews was written by Philip Yancey, in which he explains:

> Thomas Aquinas divided Jesus' teaching into Precepts and Councils, which in more modern language we might rename Requirements and Suggestions. Martin Luther interpreted the Sermon on the Mount in light of Jesus' formula "Give to Caesar what is Caesar's and to God what is God's." Christians maintain a dual citizenship, he said: one in the kingdom of Christ and one in the kingdom of the world. The extremism in the Sermon on

the Mount applies absolutely to Christ's kingdom, but not to the world's. Therefore, a Christian soldier, say, must carry out orders to fight and kill even while following Christ's law of love for enemies in his heart. In Luther's day, various Anabaptist movements chose a radically different approach. All such attempts to water down Jesus' straightforward commands are misguided, he said. Had not the early church cited Christ's commands to "love your enemies" more often than any other during its first four centuries? Simply read the Sermon on the Mount. Jesus does not differentiate between Precepts and Counsels, or the office and the person. Dispensationalists explained such teaching as the last vestige of the age of the Law, soon to be displaced by the age of Grace after Jesus' death and resurrection. Hence we need not follow its strict commands. Still another interpretation came from Albert Schweitzer, who saw the Sermon on the Mount as a set of interim demands for unusual times. Convinced that the world would soon end in the apocalypse, Jesus was setting into motion a kind of "Martial Law." Since the world did not end, we must now view his instructions differently. [1]

Though I have come to understand and study many different interpretations, my belief still holds that the sermon was meant to be lived out in Christ.

The Beatitudes: A Way to Live

I started attending a Christian college to become an elementary school teacher. One of the elective classes I quickly signed up for was on the Sermon on the Mount. Because it was a summer intensive and a small class, my friends in the class and I came up with a compelling way to interpret the Sermon on the Mount, using the Beatitudes as an outline. Though many books have been written and many teachings disseminated about this beloved message, I have found that the way we interpreted the passages in this class presents a usable and fresh application of the eight Beatitudes.

Having been a teacher for much of my life, I have found the Beatitudes to be an outline to apply these lessons as a way to live, as a practical model for preaching and teaching the Sermon on the Mount, and as the material for this book.

As a pastor and teacher, I find that for material to be concise, a good outline is essential. I always teach with notes, for fear that I might wander down some wrong path, never to return. The Sermon on the Mount begins with the eight Beatitudes laid out in a sequential order as the New Testament proclamation of eight new lessons. I have read books that outlined the eight Beatitudes and never mentioned the rest of the sermon; still others have studied the sermon, passing over the eight Beatitudes as simply nice statements or random ideas.

The last of the eight Beatitudes states, *"Blessed are the persecuted for theirs is the kingdom of heaven"* (Matthew 5:10). Immediately following this Beatitude, the verses in Matthew 5:11-20 explain what it means to be persecuted for the sake of righteousness—it will be because of Christ—and will result in our being light and salt in a very needy world.

The law will not pass away, and, unless our righteousness surpasses that of the Pharisees, we will not enter the kingdom of heaven. The teaching encapsulates what it means to be persecuted, and the qualifications for entering the kingdom, as the Beatitudes declare. The teaching was not just another set of rules to be followed, but rather a way of drawing hearers into a deeper relationship with Jesus.

The teaching in the sermon continues to change thoughts and subjects by addressing false interpretations that have developed over the years. "You have heard that it was said to people long ago…" will begin many further explanations of the sermon.

This section is where we discover a way to interpret the Sermon on the Mount as eight points (Beatitudes), using the passages in the sermon and drawing upon natural divisions to help unpack the outline of the Beatitudes. What makes my interpretation different is the realization that inverting the Beatitudes creates an order that uses the body of the sermon to explain the Beatitudes to its conclusion.

By inverting the Beatitudes, readers can see the next one in Matthew's order: *"Blessed are the peacemakers for they will be called sons of God"* (Matthew 5:9). The previous section, ending with the clarification of persecution, will now change subjects, beginning with verse twenty-one. In saying *"You have heard that it was said…"* (Matthew 5:21), Jesus clearly expresses that if your brother is at odds with you, go out of your way to make peace—be a peacemaker.

The Sermon on the Mount has an outline with these eight blessed examples that in an inverted order give clarity to the sermon. The eight Beatitudes will even summarize the message with a declarative conclusion.

A^1: *Blessed are the poor in spirit, for theirs is the kingdom of heaven.* Matthew 5:3
A^1 Explanation: Matthew 7:7-12

B^1: *Blessed are those who mourn, for they will be comforted.* Matthew 5:4
B^1 Explanation: Matthew 7:1-6

C^1: *Blessed are the meek, for they will inherit the earth.* Matthew 5:5
C^1 Explanation: Matthew 6:19-34

D^1: *Blessed are those who hunger and thirst for righteousness, for they will be filled.* Matthew 5:6
D^1 Explanation: Matthew 6:1-18

D: *Blessed are the merciful, for they will be shown mercy.* Matthew 5:7
D Explanation: Matthew 5:38-48

C: *Blessed are the pure of heart, for they will see God.* Matthew 5:8
C Explanation: Matthew 5:27-37

B: *Blessed are the peacemakers, for they will be called sons of God.* Matthew 5:9
B Explanation: Matthew 5:21-26

A: *Blessed are those who are persecuted because of righteousness, for theirs is the kingdom of heaven.* Matthew 5:10
A Explanation: Matthew 5:11-20

The eight Beatitudes listed in their inverted order correspond with a clarification found within the Sermon on the Mount. This is called a "chiasm", using the Beatitudes as the sermon's outline. (See Appendix A.)

Both the first and eighth Beatitudes speak of aspects of blessing concerning the kingdom of heaven. After the eighth lesson (Beatitude) comes the concluding remarks and application—a teaching that was amazing and left the crowd wondering about their present leadership's authority and passion for truth.

Twenty Feet

I have lived in or around water all my life. Swimming pools, boats, lakes, baths, and oceans play a large role in leisure and daily living for me.

Reading through the Genesis account of the biggest life-changing flood ever recorded, I was reminded that there is physical as well as spiritual drowning. While running from God, I often experienced a drowning feeling. The pressure around me seemed real enough, as I tried to stay afloat with all my personal resources, abilities, and time.

The Genesis account of the flood gives us some notion of the flood's depth and enormity. The Genesis account was kept for Noah and the world to realize how deep the waters were above the mountain peaks. The culmination is described in the following way:

> *The waters rose and increased greatly on the earth, and the ark floated on the surface of the water. They rose greatly on the earth, and all the high mountains under the entire heavens were covered. The waters rose and covered the mountains to a depth of more than twenty feet. Every living thing that moved on the earth perished—birds, livestock, and wild animals, all the creatures that swarm over the earth and all mankind* (Genesis 7:20-22).

Humanity was only twenty feet short; that was all the difference between life and death. Twenty feet does not seem like all that much, yet the reality of the passage is both startling and sobering. Twenty feet of water prevented people from surviving the judgment of God. All of the earth's inhabitants, local or otherwise, except for Noah and his family, drowned by a mere twenty feet.

Today, people are still without a means to escape drowning. We paddle for all we are worth, trying to outlive each other, to swim farther than our neighbors, to collect more stuff than our friends. The ultimate truth is that we are all terminal—and we are all still twenty feet short. We need an ark, and a place of safety—a means of keeping us from drowning.

The Sermon on the Mount, through its inverted order, supplies an outline by which we can keep from drowning. Christ is our ark. Noah floated to safety; Moses floated to the arms of the pharaoh's daughter; even Jonah was kept from drowning by God's miraculous grace.

Yes, we are all drowning, but there is a way to swim in these dark and deep waters, to fortify our boats against the storms, and to carry ourselves into the kingdom of heaven!

Twenty Feet Deep forms the title for this book and the basis for why the Sermon on the Mount kept me from drowning. It is my hope that they will keep others from drowning as well.

When Your Boat Springs a Leak

Blessed are those who are persecuted because of righteousness, for theirs is the kingdom of heaven. Matthew 5:10

Explanation: Matthew 5:11-20

A beautiful day marked the beginning of our annual family camping trip. We had been going for several years to Silverwood Lake Recreational Area, a Southern California camping site. My children were with me as we prepared for a week of boating, swimming, and camping. I made a quick check that everything was ready, including verifying that the plug was in the boat.

We launched our boat and powered over to our rented slip. After securing the boat, we headed back to our campsite for a light breakfast.

About two hours later, as we were walking back to the dock, my son asked a question that very well may be a boater's worst nightmare: "Dad, where is our boat?" I was only half listening as I glanced in the direction of our dock. Cluttering the debris field in the water were life jackets, a few skis, and a pair of gloves. Right where a twenty-foot craft had been was the bow of the boat, about eighteen inches out of the water, complete with navigation lights. As the boat manufacturer had promised, the boat would not sink—at least not completely.

A few hours later, we would discover that the plug, which had once been in its rightful place, had not been tightened down. In a little over an hour, a one-inch hole had allowed my boat to sink—along with our hopes for a great week.

Several times the disciples faced their boat's inability to stay afloat. When the floodwaters rose over the earth—over the highest mountaintop—twenty feet became the difference between living and drowning. The ark, God's boat, was the only structure that could carry Noah and his family to safety. Recognizing that no one will be able to keep from sinking when our boats lose their battle to bring men safely to shore, we know that Jesus will be the only means to stay afloat.

When Jesus comes to you walking on the water or He asks you to come to Him, you realize that boats sink without the Savior. And, when you have sprung a leak, your hope of survival can be found in the lessons of the Beatitudes.

Congratulations

To this day, the Sea of Galilee is surrounded by fertile lands within a moderate climate in a beautiful part of Israel. The only freshwater lake in the area, the Sea of Galilee served as an attraction for the establishment of small villages that once dotted the countryside and hills. They grew olives, figs, and dates, and enjoyed a prosperous fishing trade.

Along with these small villages, the Roman city of Tiberius was built. Jews avoided the Roman cities, instead traveling and trading with Jewish towns and attending their synagogues. The village of Capernaum has a synagogue still standing today with foundation stones that date from the time of Christ.

Jesus, a teacher from that area, spent most of his ministry in Galilee. It was on those rolling hills, sweeping slowly down toward the lake, that Jesus gave the Sermon on the Mount. From the eight Beatitudes and their amazing explanation, this teaching keeps us from drowning when water rises above our heads or when our boat takes in so much water that sinking seems inevitable. These lessons secure our lives to Him, and ensure that no matter the storms of life that come against us, we shall have no fear of drowning.

The word "blessed" is often defined as happy or joyful. Glen Stassen remarks,

> "These teachings are called The Beatitudes because they begin with the Greek word makarioi (beatus in Latin), meaning blessed, happy, hopeful, or joyful."[2]

In my study, I prefer the associations evoked by joyful, and therefore regard the word "blessed" to mean "one to be congratulated." Jesus says, *"Blessed are those who are persecuted for righteousness"* (Matthew 5:10). So you could say, "Happy are you when these things happen," or "Congratulations on your persecution. You should be so happy"! Jesus is telling us that such "congratulations" happen every day that you live righteously. Every day you do something upright, you can hear the heavens say, "Congratulations, this is how you were meant to live." We must listen for our congratulations—not from men, but from God.

Port Persecution and Giving Thanks

Blessed are you when people insult you, persecute you and falsely say all kinds of evil against you because of me. Rejoice and be glad, because great is your reward in heaven, for in the same way they persecuted the prophets who were before you. Matthew 5:11-12

My boat sank as it floated in port. Likewise, sometimes we do not get very far in our journey of faith before our spiritual boat springs a leak.

Matthew, written from the Jewish perspective of establishing the Kingdom of God, encourages an understanding that storms of persecution will come. Matthew 5:11 begins to explain what this means and how persecution can sink even the most seaworthy vessel.

Persecution is different for every individual—it can come when we least expect it and from multiple fronts. In my mind, persecution is when I have to wait in a long line or if my car has a flat tire.

However, the kind of persecution that can cause a boat to take on water is not only about hardships or mishaps in life, but about living for Christ. In the book Kingdom Ethics, the authors state:

> The Beatitudes should be interpreted in the context of the prophets with their emphases on God's reign and God's call for righteousness and justice, and the suffering that they bore for calling Israel to covenant fidelity in their own day. As Matthew 5:17-20 makes clear, Jesus is teaching in continuity with the Law and the Prophets. In a nutshell, blessed are those who suffer because of their practices of loyalty to Jesus and to justice. [3]

Jesus again reminds the crowd, *"Rejoice and be glad, because great is your reward in heaven"* (Matthew 5:11). Heaven is where our reward is kept, and any true persecution reminds us that this world is not our home.

Heaven is our ultimate destination. Rejoicing becomes a way of life for the persecuted!

One way to stop the flow of water into a sinking boat is to find the source of the leak. Persecution from living righteously can become the source that threatens to sink your boat. However, this persecution comes with a promise—this world is not our home, it is not our final reward, and the last word has not been spoken. Jesus will keep safe that which we offer to Him.

Rejoicing creates the understanding that we are fulfilling the way people were created to live. Jesus will not allow us to go down with the ship, but through our rejoicing, will keep us safe at both sea or in port. Persecution stemming from righteousness will become a way of life.

We are supposed to have some form of holiness, a standard that keeps us different from those who have no hope. After my boat sank during our family vacation, it was repaired—but eventually I needed to sell it. Should I have put a sign on it that read, "Rarely used as a submarine?" Or, stated that it runs as good under the water as on top of it? Being honest in our dealings with others quickly sets us apart. Honesty and character will not necessarily bring persecution, but because of Jesus, as with the prophets, we should speak the truth and be ready for a storm.

The rocks on a shoreline can spell disaster for any boater. The rocks of our persecution can become traps or barriers preventing us from safe arrival into port. I am amazed at how the small rocks in our lives can become great obstacles to living righteously.

A few years back, we were gathering electronic gear for a trip to Africa. I gave a cashier $520 for a $519 bill and she gave me back change of around $80 dollars. Though I had given her a $20 dollar bill, she insisted it was a $100 dollar bill. I pointed out her mistake and she proceeded to argue with me. The purchases were for our missions trip and here we were being given $80 that was not ours to take. We really could have used it, but I insisted that she recount her money. She reluctantly counted out the money and she found that we were right.

Events and interactions that occur in our every day life will invite us to consider things like which road to take or whether or not we should swim to shore on our own. Persecution will come when we choose to sail our boats with Jesus on board and in charge. Thus, when we hear the words "blessed are you" or "congratulations", we understand something about righteousness and persecution. It does not say, "Blessed are you who are persecuted for doing something dumb," nor does it say, "Blessed are you when you're persecuted for being weird." It does not even say, "Blessed are you because you have a hard time living a holy life." The Bible simply states we are blessed when we are persecuted because of righteousness—because of our love for Jesus.

Along these lines, as David Martyn Lloyd-Jones explains,

> "Being righteous, practicing righteousness, really means being like the Lord Jesus Christ. Therefore, they are blessed who are persecuted for being like Him." [4]

Righteousness means I am engaging the lifestyle of the society in which I find myself. Thus, if we live in the kingdom of heaven, we live according to the kingdom and we act according to the laws of our King.

We cannot imitate—we cannot be like Jesus—on our own. We need to be transformed, and changed by recognizing what Christ has done on our behalf. Something must happen in you for Christ to work through you. In that distinction there are three words to remember: *"...because of Me"* (Matthew 5:11). Remember that when Paul—who was then Saul—persecuted the church, he was instrumental in putting people to death because of their Christian faith. Jesus blinded Saul, put him on the ground, and asked, *"Saul, Saul, why do you persecute Me?"* (Acts 9:4).

Jesus is in the boat with us! When we are persecuted, He takes it very personally, as if He is the one being persecuted. We must give thanks to God no matter the storm. Rejoice and be glad, because your reward is in heaven. When we rejoice through the inevitable persecutions, we prove that we are like Christ.

The world cannot wait for the weekend, and even thanks God for Fridays. I overheard some neighbors, when asked, "What did you do this weekend"? respond with, "I got so drunk, I could not remember where I parked my car." After listening to their conversation, I reflected that it was as if they were without direction and their boat was taking on water. They were drowning and did not even know it. They continued by relating all the things they had done, much of which does not bear repeating.

When was the last time you heard someone at work, or in your neighborhood, when asked about their weekend, respond by saying, "Oh, I went to church and had an amazing encounter with God. My life was changed and I slept with a clear conscience." Many would be persecuted and ridiculed for recounting such an experience. We have become targets in this world, and Jesus reminds us of that truth. You will be persecuted, but when it is because of our new life in Him… rejoice!

Exposure and Service

You are the salt of the earth. But if the salt loses its saltiness, how can it be made salty again? It is no longer good for anything, except to be thrown out and trampled by men. You are the light of the world. A city on a hill cannot be hidden. Neither do people light a lamp and put it under a bowl. Instead they put it on its stand, and it gives light to everyone in the house. In the same way, let your light shine before men, that they may see your good deeds and praise your Father in heaven. Matthew 5:13-16

In concentrated service, the source is salt. Salt can stop decay, preserve food, and sustain life. Salt helps our bodies retain fluid, which is a necessity for survival. It also is used for providing flavor, for without salt, the world's food would be quite bland. As salt adds flavor to otherwise dull food, Christians bring flavor to a dull world. Though certain sins are paraded in front of us as a means to spice up our lives, the true source of spice is salty Christians.

Jesus says, *"You are the salt of the earth"* (Matthew 5:13). Though we have no fear in our country of not getting enough salt, we still have a basic understanding of the need. We cannot live without salt. In the past, when salt was scarce, men paid in salt. In fact, salt was weighed as equal to or even more precious than gold. An old work adage was, "You aren't worth your salt"— meaning you do not perform to your potential.

The hope of humanity is the individual Christian living out his life as salt in the midst of this world. If you remove the church, you remove true life. The most concentrated substance in the world is salt—a little goes a long way. Therefore, we can be assured that just one Christian applying these lessons can make a difference. Salt will never be anything other than salt, but it can be diluted. Water it down enough, and it will lose its essence. We can become less than we are meant to be through sin, poor choices, and limited testimony. We are salt; and when we accept Christ's invitation to not drown, our lives are forever changed. No longer living in fear of drowning, we begin to notice that we have become a target for persecution.

Salt stings, it preserves, it brings life—the more pure it is, the more that salt flavors the world. Jesus said that salt can lose its saltiness and when that happens it becomes good for only one thing—*"to be thrown out and trampled on by men"* (Matthew 5:13).

What happens in this world when we say we are to be persecuted for righteousness, but somehow we allow our lives to become diluted? We will be trampled. And, what happens in today's world when those who confess they are believers—followers of Jesus Christ—commit a public sin? The ever-present media tears them apart and tramples them.

Rome had many roads to maintain all over its vast territory. Using salt was the best way to contain the weeds that grew in the road. After salting the roads, men would walk upon the salt, trampling it under their feet. People would harm enemies by salting their fields, causing their crops to wither and die so that they would be unable to replant until the salt was diluted enough.

You do not have to become salt—it is what you are in Christ. You don't work at it, as it's something that permeates us. Lose your edge and the outcome will be persecution that will not be for righteousness, but for loss of effectiveness in Christ. David Kinnaman reminds us:

> We are responsible to engage the world. Jesus uses many metaphors for this. We are the light of the world (that is, we offer guidance that points people to restoration): we are salt of the earth (we help preserve people); and we are a city on a hill (we offer protection and hope for people) (see Matthew 5:13-16). Yet calling ourselves Christians does not mean that guiding, preserving or protecting is easy and automatic. It's our duty to help remedy a broken world, but this takes effort. [5]

Jesus reveals, *"You are the light of the world. A city on a hill cannot be hidden"* (Matthew 5:14). Light reveals, illuminates, exposes. While teaching in the Galilee area, Jesus would merely have to point to the hills around the lake and people would understand that light, especially when surrounded by the dark, cannot be hidden. In light, we become conspicuous. We are the light of the world, and the greater the darkness, the greater the light. The church does not need to worry about how dark the world gets, for we are the constant source of revelation to the true light.

I have been out on the water in our boat when the ambient light no longer guided my way. Our boat is equipped with the required navigation lights, and although they do not illuminate your path, they become a point of reference and a caution to other boaters. You can see the navigation lights miles away, especially when the water reflects them. As Christians, we do not always have to shine our light in people's faces—we can help them find Jesus just by being visible. No one has to tell a boater lost at sea that they should be searching for the light. They just do so instinctively.

As the persecuted, we are salt and light. We are not to diminish in effectiveness (salt) or lose our conspicuousness (light). Our witness will draw attention and persecution against the righteousness we have in Christ.

We cannot escape that we are all going to drown, as even the highest mountaintop was not spared during the flood. To find a true lifeline is the hope of the world. What we do with this lifeline defines our future. Though my boat can take on water, Jesus remains with me, lighting my way to safety. Thus, we become a light for those who have lost their way, and to those who have found that their boats have sprung a leak as well. As darkness falls, the lights become more conspicuous. Start rejoicing, because our light cannot be hidden!

Last Christmas, my wife purchased a man-sized flashlight for me. Equipped with a million lumens, it is enough to blind yourself and half the campground. As Christians, we are the light that cannot be hidden. Light illuminates, but does not assume the characteristic of what it reveals. You can take a flashlight to a landfill and shine its revealing light over all the refuse and expose the depth of decay. However, if you turn off the light, the brokenness it had once revealed does not cling to the light.

Light is not supposed to be hidden. It will reveal the decay and brokenness of the world even as it directs mankind to a safe port. We do not need to fear the light becoming tarnished by what it reveals, for light is what we are in Christ. We recognize that we are to expose, as Jesus says, *"This is the verdict: Light has come into the world but men loved darkness instead of light because their deeds are evil"* (John 3:19).

The Charted Course

Do not think that I have come to abolish the Law or the Prophets; I have not come to abolish them, but to fulfill them. I tell you the truth, until heaven and earth disappear, not the smallest letter, not the least stroke of a pen, will by any means disappear from the Law until everything is accomplished. Anyone who breaks one of the least of these commandments and teaches others to do the same will be called least in the kingdom of heaven, but whoever practices and teaches these commands will be called great in the kingdom of heaven. Matthew 5:17-19

Jesus will catch any wandering attention with this committed statement: *"Do not think that I have come to abolish the Law or the Prophets; I have not come to abolish them, but to fulfill them"* (Matthew 5:17). The Bible offers many different examples of the prophet's law; many rules were binding and seemingly impossible to keep. The people of Israel were looking for release from the burden of the Law, for redemption from the bondage of Rome. There is Moral Law found in Exodus, as expressed through the summation called the Ten Commandments. We have found that even in keeping these commandments, many will fall short. There is also the Judicial Law, which is found in the book of Deuteronomy, and the Ceremonial Law, which is the book of Leviticus. The Talmud, the Jewish interpretation of the different laws, was added to help further define and expand upon these Laws' requirements.

It would appear that up to this point, Jesus was doing rather well in his sermon. He understood the persecuted, and if ever there were a persecuted people, it was the Jews. The Pharisees listened and might have clapped in agreement saying, "Oh that's true, that's true." He then stated, *"You are the salt of the earth"* (Matthew 5:13), which could have been followed by more clapping and heads nodding in agreement saying, "Jesus, you are so right." Then Jesus stated, *"You are the light of the world"* (Matthew 5:14), and the crowd was His to command.

Then Jesus made a statement that I believe would have caused silence: *"Think not that I have come to abolish the Law or the Prophets, but I have come to fulfill them"* (Matthew 5:17). The Pharisees most likely would have said, "What did He just say?" The sermon just turned from a good word, to a powerful word—a radical life-saving message to keep us all from certain drowning.

Jesus goes on to eliminate any doubt about what He had just said, "...*not the smallest letter, not one stroke of a pen will by any means disappear from the Law*" (Matthew 5:18), and thus the Law stands! He said that the whole of Scripture is the Word of God, and forever it will stand...every word. No matter how carefully we have constructed our lives (our boat), we are going to sink. No matter how well we swim, drowning in the deep water is assured. Jesus is very clear, so that no one will misunderstand Him. We cannot keep these laws on our own. We cannot enter into the kingdom of heaven without Jesus! Dallas Willard agrees:

> The law and the prophets had been twisted around to authorize an oppressive, though religious, social order that put glittering humans--the rich, the educated, the "well-born," the popular, the powerful, and so on--in possession of God. Jesus' proclamation clearly dumped them out of their privilege position and raised ordinary people with no human qualifications into the divine fellowship by faith in Jesus. [6]

With Jesus, we may find a way to be saved from waters that would surely drown even the best of swimmers, sink even the greatest of boaters. Jesus said, "*I have not come to abolish it...*" (Matthew 5:17), and His desire is to get into our boats and see us safely to shore. His listeners were hoping He would say, "No more Ten Commandments, no more offerings, a new day without all that old bondage is coming!" All of a sudden everybody is reeling, asking, "How can we do this?" Jesus said, "*I have not come to abolish, but I have come to fulfill*" (Matthew 5:17)!

Thank God anyone who calls on the name of Jesus Christ can learn these lessons and with His help, fulfill every requirement before God.

Keeping You Afloat

For I tell you that unless your righteousness surpasses that of the Pharisees and the teachers of the law, you will certainly not enter the kingdom of heaven. Matthew 5:20

It only took an hour or two for my boat to sink with only one hole. Consequently, the plug took on a greater importance than I had previously thought.

Our lives can easily be sunk when we do not realize the absolute need of a Savior. We can have a sense of safety from external harm—just as seat belts provide some protection as we drive, we figure our boat will keep us from drowning. No matter how well they have been constructed, all boats will eventually fail and all will be lost. As the *Titanic* was deemed unsinkable, a foolish disregard for danger cost the lives of over one thousand men, women, and children.

Matthew 5:20 commands us, *"For I tell you that unless your righteousness surpasses that of the Pharisees and the teachers of the law, you will certainly not enter the kingdom of heaven,"* which leaves us with only one possibility—find and secure the One who can keep us from drowning.

The Pharisees' righteousness was widely known. They lived as close to the Law as was humanly possible. They constructed their lives as vessels able to endure any storm. They created a way of living with purity and unrivaled sacrifice. They held to the power of the Law to keep them in right standing before God. They thought their boat could not sink!

However, Jesus challenged their abilities in spiritual shipbuilding by declaring that even their uprightness would not prevent them from sinking. Their response resembled my own upon realizing that my boat had sunk while it was tied to the dock; the magnitude of what had happened was overwhelming. When Jesus declared that there was no entrance into the kingdom without righteousness, He pointed to the only One who could save a drowning world. Twenty feet is the difference between living and drowning—and Jesus positioned himself to be the only way that men could be saved. (See John 3:17.)

It will not matter how gifted we are or what talent we have acquired—we need Jesus to keep our boats afloat. Jesus came not only to keep us from drowning, but also to help us appreciate the knowledge that we are going to live abundantly. Jesus came to correct the self-deception that we can make it to the other side on our own, and He came to fulfill the law and all of its requirements.

The first repair was the reason he had come. Jesus said, *"Just as the Son of Man did not come to be served, but to serve, and to give his life as a ransom for many"* (Matthew 20:28). The reward of the kingdom will be found in the ransom of Jesus Christ. He will make the repairs and pay the price when there seems to be no hope. Enlisting Jesus in your shipbuilding effort will assure safe sailing through life's various, but certain, storms. Through the reefs of confusion, barriers of darkness, or caves of sin, we will be well-served by the Master of the waves.

The second repair was the life we now live. Jesus declares, *"The thief comes only to steal and kill and destroy: I have come that they may have life, and have it to the full"* (John 10:10). The repair to our vessel begins in our very hearts. Jesus came to deliver us from what would at first seem as a common occurrence. However, there is another who competes for our very lives. He will fill our lifeboats with needs, actions, and desires that will only lead us to drowning, but Jesus has come to guide us toward a life well-lived, to pilot us in the right direction.

The third repair belongs to the final destination. Jesus reminds us, *"I have given you authority to trample on snakes and scorpions and to overcome all the power of the enemy: nothing will harm you. However, do not rejoice that the spirits submit to you, but rejoice that your names are written in heaven"* (Luke 10:19-20). The final destination will come courtesy of Jesus Christ. He will repair our boats to carry us in this present kingdom and even to cross the spiritual Jordan into heaven. No matter the persecution that may come, we are blessed people, knowing that our course has been charted and we will make it home.

Securing Our Future

There is nothing like looking at your boat bobbing like a cork underwater to make you feel helpless (and truly stupid) for allowing such a thing to happen. My plans had been laid out carefully and I had owned boats for years. The truth is we can never plan, prepare for, or judge ahead enough for all that comes our way.

The blessed life means more than avoiding pain and trial—it is actually sailing through them to reach our heavenly goal. Persecution will come when we follow Jesus. The closer we follow Him, the more that evil people will resolve to sink our boats. We are salt and we are light. Both will cause those around us to become uncomfortable with our very presence.

Our reward is not found here on earth, though; we are to live to make sure others know the kingdom of heaven is our final destination. We will not be able to arrive on our own. Our righteousness is as *"filthy rags"* (Isaiah 64:6). Our actions must be greater than those of the Pharisees.

Before us is the impossible task of meeting the expectations of the Sermon on the Mount. As in Genesis during the flood, we are twenty feet short and our boat is leaking. Jesus offers with His very life to repair the breach and steer us to our secure landing. His righteousness, His fulfillment, and His persecution will take our place.

Though we will never make it on our own, with Him we will make the needed repairs and secure our future. I have had my boat sink—but in more ways than one, Jesus resurrected me when I was drowning, lifting me to where I was meant to be.

LESSON TWO:

When You Need to Calm the Waters

Blessed are the peacemakers, for they will be the sons of God. Matthew 5:9

Explanation: Matthew 5:21-26

The day can start out so calm you hardly feel a breeze against your face. Many times, the deception of those first few hours can cause you to let your guard down—you assume that tranquil waters are ahead. Our boat was not far from our campsite when the wind began to pick up. The lake was not known for severe weather, but the clouds and wind seemed anything but poised to stay calm. As the minutes ticked by, the waves grew. A red flag by the dock was lifted up into the air and a patrol car began driving through the campground asking people to get their boats off the lake. A storm was coming.

Because my boat was very low profile—riding deeper than most in the water—I knew there was no time to waste. Getting my daughter into the boat with me, I headed for the boat ramp. Long before we were anywhere near the ramp, water came crashing over the front of the boat, swamping both of us. I headed the boat into the wind, and made it as far as the docks by the marina. As the boat filled quickly with water, I turned on both bilge pumps and prayed. As quickly as it had come, the storm passed and the waters turned completely placid. Though my daughter will never take another ride in a storm, we were safe and the waters returned to normal.

Jesus had to calm the waters several times when his disciples knew without a doubt that they were sinking. In the book of Mark, the disciples encounter a storm that puts the fear of drowning into all of them. *"A furious squall came up, and the waves broke over the boat, so that it was nearly swamped. Jesus was in the stern, sleeping on a cushion. The disciples woke Him and said to Him, 'Teacher don't you care if we drown?'"* (Mark 4:37-38). Jesus simply rebuked the waves and the storm's rough waters assumed a reassuring calm.

In this beatitude in Matthew 5:9, Jesus addresses the need for peace. Peace brings security and stabilizes those under pressure; the Bible declares that the birth of Jesus brings, *"...on earth peace to men"* (Luke 2:14).

Peacemakers are disciples who respond to the call of calming the waters around them. Anger unleashed is like the wind that causes waters, once calm, to suddenly become a raging storm threatening to sink our boats. The peacemaker will be listed as one of the blessed, who will be like the Master and calm the waters that can unexpectedly begin raging around us.

The Peaceable Life

Blessed means happy, joyful, and that congratulations may be in order. Peacemakers will go out of their way to make peace. When the waters are rough because of life's storms, a peacemaker will do whatever is required to make peace and calm the raging seas.

The first generation Christians found the waters rough with Rome, the Caesars, and the constant strife from the Judaizers. First of all, there was a recognized uniqueness; they knew who they were. They knew why they were alive, and they understood the commission from Christ. Character was to be valued, and it set them apart.

Second, there was a renewed living. A holy life was not an option. Throughout history people have lived above what the world requires. Ronald Wells captures just how far some have gone in making peace and living like Christ:

> In sixteenth-century Holland, the Mennonites were outlawed and, when caught, often executed. One of them, Dirk Willems, was being chased across an ice field when his pursuer broke through and fell in. In response to his cries for help, Willems returned and saved him from the waters. The pursuer was grateful and astonished that he would do such a thing but nevertheless arrested him, as he thought it his duty to do. A few days later Willems was executed by being burned at the stake in the town of Asperen. It was precisely his Christ likeness that brought on his execution. [7]

The Christians were going to live differently from others around them. It was an active effort of their wills. They also responded to the Lordship of Jesus Christ.

The book of Philippians states, *"That at the name of Jesus every knee should bow, in heaven and on earth and under the earth, and every tongue confess that Jesus Christ is Lord"* (Philippians 2:10-11). The Christians did just that—they declared that Jesus Christ was the Lord of their lives. They rejoiced that the Holy Spirit was an experienced reality who would never let them drown in any storm.

Peter, a fisherman who could not catch any fish without Jesus (I can relate to him), could raise his voice to preach and have three thousand people respond. Peter, having many times experienced fierce waves, learned to recognize this unique living by responding to the Lordship of Christ.

Knowing we are all going to come up twenty feet short leads us to total dependence on Christ. This type of discipleship should be a normal way of life. What does it mean to be called *"children of God"* (Galatians 3:26)? Jesus will show us in these teachings an absolute need of Him. When we have leaking boats or stormy waters, Jesus will give us hope that we will find safety.

Traditions

Life is formed through traditions of family and culture. Ethnic diversity, different backgrounds, and unique practices of family life all bring comfort to our lives.

One year in our home on St. Patrick's Day, everything was mysteriously green—the milk, the bread, even the dessert on that day (ice cream included). Though much older now, our children still speak of the things they had to eat and have never forgotten this tradition, even renewing it with their own kids. Christmas in our home was also filled with wonderful traditions. Driving in our car with the windows down while looking at Christmas lights and eating ice cream is a sacred family tradition.

Traditions provide the form and margins to our lives. They set us apart from others and make us unique. Our faith, rich with Christian tradition, is like a good friend who gives us security. I know of nothing that calms our fears more than the familiar. Traditions are the fabric of family, church, and society. When the waters are far from calm, we can count on traditions to help us gain peace.

However, we cannot achieve this peace on our own—we need Jesus. That is why the words and significance of what He taught to those who gathered back then, and to the reader today, must catch our attention. We will read these words over and over again in Matthew 5, *"You have heard that it was said long ago."* Jesus tells us, reminding us again, of the significance of tradition, and He changes the subject from persecution to peacemaking.

"But I say to you..." will challenge us throughout the Sermon on the Mount to accept a new tradition, a new way of believing, a new way of living. To paraphrase, Jesus tells the crowd that had gathered, "Before you were born I worked this stuff out and you have interpreted it incorrectly." Though our traditions must be valued, often they are clung to without regard to truth. Sometimes the safety and familiarity of traditions can wrongly take the place of faith. We come up with our own traditions that we adhere to unquestioningly, many of which God never intended.

Jesus is concerned about God's Law, human traditions, and the interpretation of them. To calm the raging waters, we must not assume that tradition or standard rules will apply. Jesus will cause us to live at a different level than even well kept traditions have allowed.

We are being called to calm the waters, knowing that we must be actively peaceable. Drowning marked the end for all of humanity in Genesis. Twenty feet was the only difference between death and survival, no matter how well people might be able swim.

We need an ark once again, and that ark is found in Jesus Christ. He keeps us from drowning and equips us to help others find that same truth.

We are called to believe that Jesus can save, and we are to live a life that will keep others from the fate of all who try to float, swim, or even paddle their way to safety.

This takes more than just thinking; it takes doing. Life with Jesus will require us to go out of our way to make peace and take action based upon the solid knowledge (faith) that without Christ, we will be without hope; thus, we are salt, light, and now free to become peacemakers. We will be changed and our newly accountable behavior will lead us to change. We will deal with others differently, speak more carefully, and make sure we calm the waters that are so easily stirred.

The Purpose of Peacemakers

But I tell you that anyone who is angry with his brother will be subject to judgment. Again, anyone who says to his brother, "Raca," is answerable to the Sanhedrin. But anyone who says, "You fool!" will be in danger of the fire of hell. Matthew 5:22

Do not make friends with a hot-tempered man, do not associate with one easily angered, or you may learn his ways and get yourself ensnared. Proverbs 22:24-25

Murder is taking another's life. When we first read these passages we may feel pretty good about ourselves. Most of us have not murdered and thus we may judge ourselves as being in line with the teaching. We silently compare ourselves, believing that because we have not murdered, we are not subject to judgment.

Then we begin to feel our feet lifting off secure ground and the waters rising. Jesus says, *"But I tell you anyone who is angry with his brother is subject to judgment"* (Matthew 5:22). Every time Jesus speaks the truth about tradition and further explains why we cannot make it without Him, the waters get deeper and deeper. Bonhoeffer challenges us about making peace:

His disciples keep the peace by choosing to endure suffering themselves rather than inflict it on others. They maintain fellowship where others would break it off. They renounce all self-assertion, and quietly suffer in the face of hatred and wrong. In so doing they overcome evil with good, and establish the peace of God in the midst of a world of war and hate. [8]

These principles were meant to be practiced with the knowledge that we would fall short trying to calm the waters without Him. But as Jesus has said, even what we think about others will mark us for judgment. The realization that we are sunk does not keep Jesus from reminding us, *"That whoever hears these words and puts them into practice..."* (Matthew 7:24). We cannot dismiss the Beatitudes as pleasant sayings that are not being practiced. When anger flares up and the waters are anything but calm, we must let Jesus guide us. We must come to realize that what is inside can cause great danger in stormy times and that peacemakers know that right thinking can bring calm waters.

Next, we come to the word "raca". If we call our brother or sister "raca"—or "empty-headed"—we risk judgment.[9] Raca may be translated as "helium for brains" or as "their driveway does not go all the way to the garage". Speaking of another as "raca" was answerable to the Sanhedrin, the religious judicial branch in the time of Jesus.

This newly established teaching asks us to consider carefully before we launch into insults. Like a yellow flashing light, this lesson warns us to proceed with care, for there are problems ahead. Jesus is establishing that if we insult someone, we are answerable to the court system.

When my boat sank, I was able to drain everything out and get it back into the water within a few hours. A worker at the dock came up as I was pulling into the marina and said, "You should have been here earlier, a real idiot sunk his boat right here." Being that idiot, I did not find his observation the least bit helpful. We can quickly respond to an insult, even if it is rightly deserved, and create the perfect storm.

I have been challenged from the book of James, as he rightly states, *"Be quick to listen and slow to speak"* (James 1:19). We all, at one time or another, have become the object of a less than thoughtful statement or joke, for which we have supplied the needed material. Peacemakers hesitate and realize that the individual is worth more than an offhanded remark that could land them in court. Jesus will accept nothing less than submitting our very thoughts to His will.

Jesus continues the peacemaker's effort to calm rough waters by identifying that anyone who says, *"You fool!"* comes against another's reputation and will be in danger of the fire of hell. There have been times when words about another came from my mouth and I was sure I could smell smoke! How easy it is to tear down another's reputation with a single word or a certain look. In our day, even the accusation of wrongdoing can be a career-killer, stirring the waters of a storm that will drown the best of swimmers. D.A. Carson reminds us:

> Here, Jesus moves through the accepted system to the ultimate punishment to make it clear that the judgment to be feared is indeed divine, for it is based on God's assessment of the heart and can end in the fire of hell. [10]

The judgment of hell is now attached to the person who accepts or insists that another is a fool, without concern that we might be assuming an unfounded judgment. Careful of another's reputation and guarding their very lives, we bring peace that can keep the winds of accusation from stirring the waters into waves that will sink both them and us. Blessed are you when you recognize the value of another's life.

The Practice of Peace

Therefore, if you are offering your gift at the altar and there remember that your brother has something against you, leave your gift there in front of the altar. First go and be reconciled to your brother, then come and offer your gift. Matthew 5:23-24

Peacemakers find a way to bring peace to situations even when they themselves have not contributed to the offense. We must go out of our way to make peace.

At our church, the waters between two couples were forming breakers that were sure to sink their friendship. They had come to an impasse and were unable to pacify their anger toward each other. The name-calling and accusations grew to a point where we found ourselves without a solid direction or resolution for the conflict. We had several meetings to try to reconcile them and find a peaceful solution.

One of our elders, sensing that the real issue was a monetary debt, offered this solution. "I love you both and God has blessed me. I will pay the money owed from your business dealings with each other. I beg you to be reconciled in Christ and forgive as you have been forgiven." I was speechless, for the amount was thousands of dollars, now being offered freely and with startling grace. It was as though Jesus had entered the room and brought peace to the rough waters. A great calm came upon us all, and we were able to bring about a resolution that saved the reputations of both families.

A peacemaker makes the first move, goes beyond the expected, creating peace where only stormy waters seem to exist. Jesus is changing us from being ones who bring harm to those around us with our thoughts and words, to leading us to become producers of peace and calm.

Jesus models for us that a blessed person realizes that he will drown without help. With Jesus, we become different people. We are being changed to be like our heavenly Father and Jesus will make sure we will make it to the other side with Him. It does not matter if it is crossing a lake, heading to Jerusalem, or waiting for the culmination of Heaven: Jesus will make sure we are safe.

The Problem with Anger

Therefore, if you are offering your gift at the altar, and there you remember that your brother has something against you... Matthew 5:23

This verse leaves us little choice in being reconciled. Here we are introduced to the blessed way to live. We must assume the role of the peacemaker, and leave even a church service to reconcile with an individual with whom we may have an irresolvable difference.

Jesus will press the real you to stand up. The real you is inside, what is in your heart; Jesus will address our inward and outward actions. The equal truth of faith and works can be read in the book of James. Knowledge of God must be accompanied by action. What we have faith in will work its way into how we live.

Dallas Willard reminds us that "anything goes" mindset is a mistake and compromises the price paid through Jesus Christ:

> Does this mean that these people of love earned their salvation? That they deserved their acceptance by God? Not at all. It is simply a description of the wideness of God's mercy. The idea that God works with humankind strictly on a basis of merit is a mistake—especially when that merit is defined in human terms, which is the usual case. But the idea that anything is acceptable to God is likewise a mistake. In His goodness and wisdom, God responds to the flawed efforts of flawed humankind to reach Him—by reaching them. He looks upon the heart; *"The Lord does not see as mortals see; they look on the outward appearance, but the Lord looks on the heart"* (1 Samuel 16:7). [11]

When anger separates people, they must not, and cannot, go on as if nothing is wrong. We cannot pretend any longer, as we are really being transformed into the type of disciple who seeks to calm the raging storms of relationships. The book, *"Kingdom Ethics"*, describes the peacemaker:

> Being a peacemaker is part of being surrendered to God, for God brings peace. We abandon the effort to get our needs met through the destruction of enemies. God comes to us in Christ to make peace with us; and we participate in God's grace as we go to our enemies to make peace. This is why the peacemakers "will be children of God". In a nutshell, blessed are those who make peace with their enemies, as God shows love to God's enemies. [12]

I have heard time heals all wounds, but I have found that people who are angry never resolve the anger or reconcile the relationship until someone makes the effort to become a peacemaker. Jesus is not going to adjust our attitudes or offer an easy way out. He is going to change us from the inside out, which will give us a new way to live, a new way to behave, and a new way to bring peace!

The Psalmist David declares, *"He leads us by quiet waters, He restores our souls"* (Psalm 23:2-3). We must settle matters quickly as we will not be able to get much accomplished while we are under judgment. We are now different people, and by acting upon the teachings of Jesus we bring peace to otherwise irreconcilable problems.

Conflict creates offenses, which lead to reactions, which then become personal offenses. How easy is it to be offended and how many times a day do we feel we have been wronged? We choose to be offended—we refuse to make peace by going to our offenders and reconciling. I am amazed at how burdens are carried year after year with no movement toward peace.

Anger, when kept from becoming an offense, will die. Most anger becomes fully alive once we attach it to our emotions. Anger tied to hurt is a lethal combination. When I was younger, my brother laughed at me for falling off my bike. Being hurt and then laughed at, I experienced a storm of anger, which I then unleashed without thinking. I threw a rock right at his head. It missed, but my father's spanking did not.

Anger also seems more volatile when we are tired. When tired, we become vulnerable to impulses of anger, reacting to things that we would otherwise not have noticed.

Peacemakers will be blessed when, in becoming like Christ, we settle with others we have offended and do what needs to be done—even leave a worship service to reconcile with a brother or sister.

Worship: To Be Changed

We will not be able to remain in a service for long if the Holy Spirit reminds us that things are not right with someone. Making resolution may require an email, a phone call, or a face-to-face encounter, but conviction will make us react to the storms ahead.

In worship, we sense God's presence and respond to His calling. Joshua, after being told the reason for Israel's failure at Ai, began to search tribe-by-tribe and then leader-by-leader, until he found Achan. The first thing that Joshua told them was to worship God. Joshua declared, *"My son, give glory to the Lord, the God of Israel, and give Him praise. Tell me what you have done; do not hide it from me"* (Joshua 7:19). These words had no sooner left his lips than Achan confessed with immediate acknowledgement.

As a peacemaker, learn always to be open to God in worship. Whether in service or practicing personal worship, be ready and listen for situations or relationships that need to be reconciled. Worship, and God's word will guide any who listen into action that will change storms into calm waters.

We worship to be changed. We cannot come before the Lord, day after day, and not be changed. We are being called and changed into His likeness, and the worship of God stands as the means for the transformation of our minds and actions.

The book of James reminds us *"works is dead"* (James 3:26). If we do not respond, we may not get out of some situations *"...until you have paid the last penny"* (Matthew 5:26). Choosing to live under judgment leads us to certain bondage and eventually to a jail of our own making. Whether physical or emotional, the debt must be paid.

Living a blessed life means becoming a son or daughter of God, knowing that He is guiding us in our thoughts, speech, and love for one another.

A Load Suddenly Lifted

There was once a situation in which I felt that I had been wronged—a position that I thought should have been offered to me was given to someone else. The supervisor who had blindly (in my opinion) appointed another was a friend whom I had known for years. From that moment on, I refused to speak to him or his wife. The waters were never calm or at peace.

As I sat in church one day about four years later, the Lord clearly brought his name to mind. I knew I could no longer avoid his and his wife's name or my very real feelings for them. That afternoon I called him. I told him of my hurt feelings and asked if we could be reconciled. He had no idea of his offense so it was easy for him to allow my forgiveness and to make it right between us. It was as if a debt had been paid and a load was suddenly lifted.

Like a boat, we will be pressed by waves and will not make forward progress until the storm ceases. I was at a standstill until that conflict was resolved. When you can see someone years later and not feel anger rise within you, the peace is real. I can say, without a doubt, that the still waters of peace have restored my soul.

LESSON THREE:

Floating on Lake Integrity

Blessed are the pure in heart, for they will see God. Matthew 5:8

Explanation: Matthew 5:27-37

Like other boat owners, over the years I have purchased boats from private parties or dealers. And, just as the phrase "used car salespeople" does not conjure the personification of integrity (though there are always exceptions), "buyer beware" has its own proven relevance to the phrase "used boat salespeople".

This beauty was fast and seemed like a great deal—a 22-foot ski boat with a wakeboard tower. Through my experience, I have learned that statements like "it just needs cleaning" or "it just needs a tune up" usually mean that I'm about to spend around a thousand dollars or more. Taking that accrued wisdom into account, I had been assured that the loose rudder in the back would be easily remedied with some tightened bolts. Indeed the bolts had become loose—but with a ready wrench, I brought the new toy into our welcoming home.

After the first season, the boat always took on more water than seemed normal. Sure, we were getting in and out, but the gallons that were pumped out seemed excessive to me. Never daunted, I looked, tightened, and watched, hoping to find the place of entry for that lake water.

The next summer, while my son was driving—it was great that he was driving so I could blame him—the boat seemed to be riding very low in the water. I was riding in a friend's boat and as we came up alongside my boat, our son calmly asked me, "Dad, should there be water all over the carpet of the boat? And, by the way, I can't steer the boat."

Upon inspections, we quickly determined that those loose bolts in the back had been allowing water into the boat all along because, even though they had been tightened, the fiberglass had completely deteriorated. Unfortunately, those same bolts were meant to hold the steering and rudder control. We were able to tow the boat to shore, arriving a few moments before all souls aboard would have had to abandon ship.

It would have been helpful if the former boat owner had informed me before my purchase, that there was risk of the back of the boat falling off. Integrity—whether in boat dealings or in how we treat each other— makes a difference in the believer's life. To alleviate any compromising of our ability to be guided, we, too, need as little water as possible to make its way into our "boats".

The pure of heart are those who will see in their lives, in their homes, and in their speech, the very presence of Christ.

Purity for Life

Come near to God and He will come near to you. Wash your hands you sinners and purify your hearts, you double-minded. James 4:8

With each of the Beatitudes, Jesus reminds us that those who keep them are blessed. We will address perfection in an upcoming chapter, allowing the followers of Jesus some room for daily acceptance and falling short.

"Congratulations" will encourage us to press ahead, as Paul's call to the Philippian church: *"Not that I have already obtained all this, or have already been made perfect, but I press on to take hold of that for which Christ Jesus took hold of me"* (Philippians 3:12).

The citizens of our country established happiness as a founding right worthy of pursuit. We now understand that long before the founding of the United States of America, Jesus had in mind humanity's true happiness and the most fulfilling way to live.

The blessed life is about more than financial gain or acquiring possessions. The blessed life is about swimming lessons that will keep us from drowning. We will all fall short on our own, but Jesus has given us the hope and grace that will keep us in the right boat, secure through the integrity of God.

Purity: Life without Mixture

Blessed are the pure in heart for they will see God. Matthew 5:8

This is a profound and life-altering Beatitude. The promise of seeing God will be based upon the need for integrity that begins in the heart. The promise does not depend merely upon outward actions, but also—and more importantly—upon the attitude of the heart.

The metamorphosis of a caterpillar turning into a butterfly means a change—a violent change—the very rearrangement of internal ingredients. The change that must take place is life altering: the irrevocable transformation of a caterpillar into a beautiful butterfly.

It is easy to see God in such a dramatic change, which is why Jesus told Nicodemus, *"...no one can see the kingdom of God unless he is born again"* (John 3:3). In these words, we see that change must occur in order for us to see God. Integrity of heart (purity) assures us that when the storms come and our boats are sinking, we do not need to be afraid when Jesus comes to us, for He will bring peace to the storm that threatens us.

Our lives will call for character and integrity, and we must choose to daily assess our level of purity. Whenever we allow emotions, boundaries, or rights to transgress justifiable levels, they take place on an illegitimate level. Purity of heart keeps integrity clear and above the water for all to see.

My daughter has played water polo for well over ten years. Treading water in a swimming pool over ten feet deep for forty-five minutes—with someone trying to drown you—is anything but easy. Many times she would come home with bruises all over her legs and arms and tell me that what happened above the water was only for show. The real action of the game is played under the water, where the referees cannot see. Water polo players engage on two levels—one above the water line and one below.

The parallel between the lives that others see, and the lives that are hidden, is where integrity and purity form. Even in waters where they could have drowned, my daughter's team usually prevailed because of the purity of playing above and below the water line. When we talk about character, we are talking about the purity of our own hearts.

The definition of purity is "unmixed, without alloy". So, blessed are those with unmixed motives.[13] The words of Bible characters and authors confirm the value of purity in our lives.

The Psalmist says, *"He who has clean hands and a pure heart, who does not lift his soul to an idol or swear by what is false. He will receive blessing from the Lord and vindication from God his Savior"* (Psalm 24:4-5). Paul reminds us of the value of all things pure. *"Finally brothers, whatever is true, whatever is noble, whatever is right, whatever is pure, whatever is lovely, whatever is admirable—if anything is excellent or praiseworthy— think about such things"* (Philippians 4:8-9).

In the book of James, purity is also noted to be practical, *"Religion that God our Father accepts as pure and faultless is this: to look after orphans and widows in their distress and to keep oneself from being polluted by the world"* (James 1:27). John says, *"Everyone who has this hope in Him purifies himself, just as He is pure"* (1 John 3:3), while in Revelation 21:21, we see that the pavement of heaven will be streets of pure gold!

The definition of "to see" is "to behold, gaze intently, to view with eyes wide open".[14] When we behold God with purity of heart, integrity puts us in the place where we can trust our eyes. Jesus challenges us to recognize the difference between imitation (seeing) and transformation (becoming). We cannot simply imitate; we must be transformed. Jesus is bringing us to a place where we will be open to the Word of God and recognize that we cannot be transformed without Him.

We would not be in fear of drowning if we could keep the Law and the prophet's teachings. But, even as the waters rose above the highest mountain by twenty feet, all of humanity knew that without the right boat, drowning was inevitable. The integrity of the ark's structure was able to float Noah, his family, and the animals to safety.

What we are seeking should come from a pure heart, as it is this grace that keeps us looking to Jesus. As Peter was sinking in the stormy lake waters, looking to Jesus kept him from drowning. Likewise, until we are safe, we must keep our eyes on Jesus as well. Lifesaving 101 always includes CPR, which translates in our spiritual lives into Christ's Personal Resources, a gift that is always available to keep us from drowning.

Integrity will keep us in whatever place we find ourselves—above, below, or in the water—able to see the Lord with pure hearts and know that He is right in front of our eyes.

Depraved Minds

Above all else, guard your heart, for it is the wellspring of life. Proverbs 23:4

Purity of heart involves integrity in three areas that Jesus applies through the explanation of Matthew 5:27-37. Firstly, purity of heart speaks to lust. Secondly, purity of heart involves the integrity needed in marriage, which Jesus shows through His addresses on divorce. Thirdly, purity of heart involves making oaths and gaining honor by keeping your word.

Purity of heart begins with the integrity of our thoughts; however, our minds are flawed. *"As a man thinks, so he is"* (Proverbs 23:7) establishes that purity begins in the mind, but *"our minds are darkened"* (Romans 1:28). Paul continues in the book of Romans, saying, *"Furthermore, since they did not think it worthwhile to retain the knowledge of God, He gave them over to a depraved mind, to do what ought not to be done"* (Romans 1:28). Paul confirms in 2 Corinthians that, *"The god of this age has blinded the minds of unbelievers, so that they cannot see the light of the gospel of the glory of Christ, who is the image of God"* (2 Corinthians 4:4).

Our minds have been darkened by impurity and the loss of seeing God through the blindness of this age, which is unbelief. We must respond to the storms that threaten our boat's integrity with purity of heart, which will keep us seeing God while He works out His purpose in our lives.

While boating on many lakes, at times I have needed to find my way while at the same time knowing the exact speed we are making on the water. Handheld Global Positioning Systems are things to marvel over. Thirty years ago, such technology would have been something out of a science fiction movie. Though we cannot see them, feel them, or taste them, we know that all around us are millions of information bits swirling throughout the airwaves. The GPS can tell your position, speed, and time. Though we cannot see their connections with the naked eye, the radio, GPS, and cell phone lock onto a satellite or a tower's frequency and download the needed information.

Our minds are not unlike these devices, in that they can tune in to spiritual frequencies. We can tune our thoughts, our eyes, and our ears toward purity or impurity. We have been created to gain knowledge and grow in integrity through our senses. If we could not see, touch, taste, smell, or hear, we would be without knowledge, without understanding. We choose with our senses to seek righteous or unrighteous things and quickly realize that our hearts could allow us to swim an unsafe distance from shore.

People have drowned in very shallow water, so the depth of one's impurity may seem safe for the moment. But integrity will not allow for "just a little purity". Only a life turned over to Jesus Christ will help us find solid footing as the waters rise. We must have spiritual integrity—our own GPS, so to speak—so that even on the lake, we will know where we are and how to find calm waters.

Dynamic Minds

Purity of mind is formed by the renewal of the mind by the Spirit of God. A renewed mind, as Paul states in Romans, means, *"Do not conform any longer to the pattern of this world, but be transformed by the renewing of your mind"* (Romans 12:2). A dynamic mind is a Christ-centered mind, as Paul declared when he said, *"We demolish arguments and every pretension that sets itself up against the knowledge of God and we take captive every thought, to make it obedient to Christ"* (2 Corinthians 10:5).

A pure mind will tune into what is righteous or pure, and will seek what will build up the listener. Purity begins in the mind and finds its way to the heart. Paul, teaching young Timothy, expresses this truth by saying, *"Train yourself to be godly"* (1 Timothy 4:7). Training, pressing, and spiritual transformation start in the mind and heart. Dallas Willard believes that to love God is to have Him constantly before you, and he notes:

> The love of God, and only the love of God, secures the
> vision of God, keeps God constantly before our mind.

Thomas Watson tells us the "the first fruit of love is the musing of the mind upon God. He who is in love, his thoughts are ever upon the object. He who loves God is ravished and transported with contemplation of God . . . God is the treasure, and where the treasure is, there is the heart." King David gives us the secret of his life: *"I keep the Lord always before me; because He is at my right hand, I shall not be moved."* (Psalm 16:8) [15]

Impure actions and motives cannot find balance with true purity. Actions and motives must be "without mixture". The heart becomes the seat of the Holy Spirit, the guardian of our hearts in Christ. When our senses send information or knowledge that has been tuned into the Holy Spirit, He will then guard and guide the response. If it is impure, He will persuade us to let it go.

If through our will we override His conviction, what we experience through our senses will journey from our hearts to our minds. Thus, we become what we think or dwell upon, so the heart must seek to see the Lord in purity.

The pure of heart will seek integrity in their lives, in their homes, and in their speech. Living as followers of Christ, we will be more connected to each of these areas of accountability than we might ever have dreamed possible. Our very thoughts can become snares to impure motives, rendering us in need of forgiveness. Swimming or boating will bring storms in which decisions must be made about how pure we desire our hearts to be. Christ will keep us in Him, and the pure will see Him up close!

Lust: The Adulterous Heart

You have heard that is was said, "Do not commit adultery." But I tell you that anyone who looks at a woman lustfully has already committed adultery with her in her heart. If your right eye causes you to sin, gouge it out and throw it away. It is better for you to lose one part of your body that for your whole body to be thrown into hell. And if your right hand causes you to sin, cut it off and throw it away. It is better for you to lose one part of your body than for your whole body to go into hell. Matthew 5:27-30

The desire for something that will lead from a legitimate emotional level to an illegitimate action always begins with the heart. Simply put, lust equals a form of unbelief.

Looking at another woman and thinking that your marriage would be different if you had some kind of relationship with her, instead of with the person you are married to, will create a heart full of unbelief. When one is not married, lust becomes the lurking desire that promises far more than it will ever deliver. Lust is looking at what someone else owns and saying, "If I had that, I would be more fulfilled." Craig S. Keener states this about adultery:

> Adultery usually involves considerable rationalization, justifying one's behaviors as necessary of loving; but lust is the mother of adultery, the demonic force that allows human beings to justify exploiting one another sexually, at the same time betraying the most intimate of commitments where trust ought to abide secure even where it can flourish, nowhere else. Lust demands possession, love, value, respect, and seeks to serve other persons with what is genuinely good for them. Lust is always incompatible with acknowledging God as the supreme desire of our hearts, because it is contrary to His will. [16]

Lust implies that what God has given us cannot provide fulfillment and will never be enough. Lust is unbelief. Tuning our hearts to praise God creates peace and thankfulness that comes with pure contentment.

Jesus could not be more serious about the danger of lust to faith. The heart provides the stability that keeps us afloat and swimming in the right direction. Integrity translates into the practical application of the eye and hand.

Jesus speaks about adultery not only in reference to marriage, but also regarding people who could be adulterous to God. *"If your eye offends you, pluck it out. If your right hand causes you to sin, cut it off"* (Matthew 5:29). The literal interpretation of that scripture would leave the church blind and unable to pass any offering plates! I can remove my eyes but still have lust in my heart. Interpreting these words spiritually will leave the reader with some good thoughts, but with no real means of applying the teaching, which certainly limits the results.

Many times when swimming with my family, I have warned my children of dangers in the water. Many things below the surface are not visible, thus to dive in headfirst can have life-altering results. "I have told you a million times not to do that" is an exaggeration for a hopeful affect. Jesus warns us of the serious consequences of unchecked lust. These consequences should be so feared, that if we cannot control the lust, then radical responses become necessary. If it can save you, then the response is worth the pain and life-altering experience. Eugene Peterson, in his book *Under the Unpredictable Plant*, speaks of lust after another's ministry:

> Parish glamorization of ecclesiastical pornography-taking photographs (skillfully airbrushed) or drawing pictures of congregations that are without spot or wrinkle, the shapes that a few parishes have for a few short years. These provocatively posed pictures are devoid of personal relationships. The pictures excite a lust for domination, for gratification, for uninvolved and impersonal spirituality. [17]

Again, the only way to have a truly pure life is to hold Jesus in front of our eyes, guiding our hands. Purity and integrity begin in the heart, and the pure heart remains ever the goal of those who know that only in Christ, can we be changed from the inside out.

Guard your heart from impurity and lust—and hold fast to John's words in the book of Revelations, which say, *"What you have seen and what you have heard, guard against those things that can corrupt"* (Revelation 3:3).

Divorce: The Afflicted Home

It has been said, "Anyone who divorces his wife must give her a certificate of divorce." But I tell you that anyone who divorces his wife, except for martial unfaithfulness, causes her to become an adulterous, and anyone who marries the divorced woman commits adultery. Matthew 5:31-32

Integrity must permeate every area of our lives so that it infiltrates our every thought and act. On the subject of divorce, we must face Jesus' teachings, which cannot be ignored or glossed over as if He were just dispensing a few impractical suggestions. We must apply His lessons without condemnation, realizing that to fulfill any part of the sermon, we need Jesus to help us. As in the days of Jesus, marriages remain in far deeper water than we can even imagine. While many different statistics have shown that over fifty-percent of marriages end in divorce, a great need persists to consider the purity of the home.

The Bible gives us principles that we should prayerfully and intelligently apply to every situation. We think marriage is like a brand-new boat—new upholstery, new motor, and everything works perfect. But marriage, in my opinion, is more like buying an old used boat—it needs paint, the tires on the trailer need replacing, and the motor needs to be rebuilt. Everything is there, but we face the job of choosing the best course of action to build this vessel as a couple.

After ten years, we will find that the marriage reveals evidence of our touch and bears our signature; the repairs laced with all the hard-earned work have become our investment. Marriage takes time even with both people working together toward a common goal.

Any project takes longer than we had planned, costs more than we had thought, and makes more of a mess than we had anticipated. However, it is worth the wait and the work to see what we will build with the help of our partner. Divorce rates escalate—in spite of volumes of teaching materials, resources, marriage encounters, and an untold number of books.

Many people reading these words may have already experienced a divorce. The realization that God forgives all things brings hope—but remember, even divorce begins with the heart. If people would repent and vow never to turn down the path of divorce again, we would see far fewer homes impacted by multiple marriages, each ending in divorce. We would see many marriages saved if the hearts of both husband and wife were to seek God in purity.

What we fail to accomplish in faith will end in unbelief. This situation will not improve without a changed heart and the realization that without Christ in the boat with us, we are sinking. Realizing that none of us will make it without Christ puts our failures into perspective; we do not need to have our failures thrown into our faces, adding condemnation to an already deep hurt. The ideal of marriage remains the biblical truth, the foundation of the family. Jesus neither diminishes its value nor ranks it in order of importance. Purity of heart is needed to overcome lust in the heart and affliction in the home.

Oath: The Admirable Honor

Again, you have heard that it was said to people long ago, "Do not break your oath, but keep the oaths you have made to the Lord." But I tell you, do not swear at all: either by heaven, for it is God's throne; or by the earth, for it is His footstool; or by Jerusalem, for it is the city of the Great King. And do not swear by your head, for you cannot make even one hair white or black. Simply let your 'Yes' be 'Yes,' and your 'No', 'No'; anything beyond this comes from the evil one. Matthew 5:33-37

The third area taught within our purity of heart, is the articulation of an oath and admirable honor. We go to court and are told to tell the truth, the whole truth, and nothing but the truth. What has developed over the years becomes very clear—we have little concept of truth and our speaking has become somewhat "truth-less". Dietrich Bonhoeffer said these words about the nature of the oath:

> The very existence of oaths is a proof that there are such things as lies. If lying were unknown, there would be no need for oaths. Oaths are intended as a barrier against untruthfulness. But it goes further than that; for there, where alone the Oaths claim final truth, is space in life given to the lie, and it is granted a certain right of life. [18]

When I purchased the boat that had rotting fiberglass, only a partial truth was revealed. Integrity seems to be more in levels than in a single measurable standard. The teaching in this sermon will remind us of how we are to live as forgiven individuals. The waters of integrity sometimes may not seem very inviting—but when we pursue with purity of speech, we find a way to stay above the storms and keep ourselves floating with integrity toward port.

There is no truth in God without truth toward people. Among the most important lessons we find recorded in the Old Testament are when people gave their word. In the book of Joshua, the Gibeonites deceive the Israelites with their worn-out clothes and food supplies, allowing them to believe they came from a great distance. Though lying, the Gibeonites would be in a protected relationship with the Israelites. Though deceived, Joshua and the elders could not back out—they gave their oath.

Jesus said, *"Let your 'yes' be 'yes' and your 'no' be 'no'"*... (Matthew 5:37), and there is no room for anything else. In this teaching, Jesus addresses that people were adding to what they were saying with a heavenly agreement—"I swear by heaven." Sorry, Jesus says, that is God's throne room. "Well then, I swear by earth." Sorry, that is His footstool. "Okay, then I swear by my head." Sorry, that is not acceptable, because you cannot make one hair white or black. You cannot change anything.

Where can we go that God is not already there? We can say nothing that God has not already heard. That is why it is wrong to take taking God's name in vain—frivolously or evasively swearing—or taking God's name and making it binding. Heaven is the throne of God, and the earth is His footstool, and Jerusalem is the city of God. Life cannot be divided into places where God is and God is not.

When our hands are doing what God wants us to do, we will touch God. When our eyes are seeing what God wants us to see, we will see God. When our hearts are pure, we change how we think about lust and we walk with honor, keeping vows we have made.

My father came from a handshake world. He would look someone in the eye and ask, "Do you give me your word?" His word was his bond: that was always enough for him. When I asked my wife to marry me, my father told me that the greatest gift I will give my wife is my name. "Your name is all you are, all you have to give." I have never forgotten those words, and I remember there is nothing to be added when I give my word. My heart, my marriage, and my oaths are witnessed by God even before I speak them. Nothing more is needed.

Integrity can be the word for both the character and the condition of a boat. If the integrity of the hull is solid, the boat will float. If there is a stress fracture or fiberglass failure, the boat will not remain on top of the water.

The blessed life does not come about by wishful thinking or by trying to stay afloat, as Noah must have encouraged his friends to try. We all are going to drown unless we find a way to get to land safely.

Jesus will meet you and change you from the inside out. The Sermon on the Mount, as outlined by the Beatitudes, reminds us of the integrity that begins with the heart. The pure of heart—those without mixture—will see God at work in their lives. He will begin by dealing with lust, confronting our marriages about divorce, and holding us to our words as we make oaths.

Each of these Beatitudes comes with powerful words of explanation and instructions that we are called upon to keep. When we fail, there is forgiveness, for the Savior will take His place in the boat, in the water, or wherever we may find ourselves without hope.

LESSON FOUR:
The Merciful Boater

Blessed are the merciful, for they will be shown mercy. Matthew 5:7

Explanation: Matthew 5:38-48

The words "mercy" and "forgiveness" are multifaceted. We are asked to grant forgiveness for everything–from harshly spoken words, to a murderer who robbed us of a loved one. Forgiveness seems to have fallen on hard times. How can mercy be extended when the action against us is so life-altering?

To live above the world's standard of recognized acceptance, the Christian must decide whether to be different in dealings with others. It is hard to imagine how many times, as followers of Christ, we are asked, "What would Jesus do?" We wish, of course, that we knew exactly the right response for every violation we have received, but Jesus only gives us a compass, not a map, to navigate the path of living and following Him as a model for spiritual discipleship. Willard reminds us,

> "The correct perspective is to see following Christ not only as the necessity it is, but as the fulfillment of the highest human possibilities and as life on the highest plan." [19]

While camping with my family, our twelve-year-old daughter was accompanying me to the dock to fill up our boat with gas. There are moments when time stands still—drifting into slow motion—and you wish you could retrace the past few seconds. That moment was soon coming.

We were not alone on the lake that day, as there was one other boater out for an early morning tube run with his family. They were weaving back and forth across the lake, oblivious that anyone else might be out on the water. I started to leave the dock, then quickly began making defensive moves to avoid the other boater. He was looking behind him, watching his kids on their tubes. Not one person in the boat was looking forward.

I stopped, turned, made corrections, and began to think that this guy should not own a boat! As we picked up speed and headed the other direction, their boat made a completely unexpected turn and was headed straight for us. There was nothing I could do—no amount of maneuvering would stop what was about to happen.

Their boat went right over the left side of our boat, removing the backside of my engine cover and ski pole. My daughter was sitting behind me where the boat hit us and proceeded to go airborne right over us. The two-and-a-half inch stainless steel ski pole had bent to a ninety-degree angle and miraculously spared my daughter of any serious injury. She had only a small scrape on her arm and otherwise was untouched. The other boater received some minor scratches and a few sore ribs, but he had no idea what he had hit! He was ticketed for reckless boating and both of our boats were a total loss.

Though my daughter was safe, mercy had to be offered to this person who nearly killed us both. In order for that to happen, I was going to need a little more perfecting than I presently had attained. "Blessed are the merciful" was about to become very personal to me. God reminded me that when I was drowning from my own sin, mercy was given to me, and forgiveness offered. Boating and mercy began to take on a whole new meaning. With the ultimate question of how we should live out our lives, the Beatitudes depict a life well lived. Lloyd-Jones defines the blessed person as one who is not confused about character:

> The only man who is at all capable of carrying out the injunctions of the Sermon on the Mount is the man who is perfectly clear in his mind with regard to the essential character of the Christian. Our Lord says that this is the only kind of person who is truly "blessed", that is "happy". Someone has suggested that it might be put like this; this is the sort of person who is congratulated, this is the sort of person to be envied, for they alone are truly happy. [20]

"Blessed are the merciful for they shall receive mercy" (Matthew 5:7) is one of the key lessons to an extraordinary life.

A World in Need of Mercy

We must realize that extending mercy is the way to say, "Yes!" when the world shouts, "No!" The merciful will be shown mercy, for when you have need of extended grace, what you have expended to others will be the measure of grace shown to you. Willard describes the difference between the merciful and the world's perception:

The worldly wise will, of course, say, "Woe to the merciful, for they shall be taken advantage of." And outside heaven's rule there is nothing more true. My mother and father went bankrupt and lost their clothing business in the early 1930's, just before I was born. Those were depression years, and they simply could not make people pay for what they needed. Clothing was given "on credit" when it was clear there would be no payment. A familiar story, no doubt. The merciful are always despised by those who know how to "take care of business". Yet outside the human order, under the great profusion of heaven's goodness, they themselves find mercy to meet their needs, far beyond any "claim" they might have on God. [21]

Mercy is the realization that you need something extended from God that cannot be earned or merited. Mercy is God's rescue of people lost in sin and unforgiveness towards one another. When we are a long way from shore and our boat is being rocked by the waves of life, it is easy to lose perspective. While floating in my kayak, a speeding powerboat going by has left me a five-foot wake to contend with and such action does not appear to be showing mercy to the smaller vessel! The careless acts of other people can make many waves to rock our boats. Though life is filled with many waves and storms, God desires to guide and rescue us through His mercy with the expectation that we will do the same turn to others. The book Kingdom Ethics reminds us that our mercy must not be limited to friends:

> The transforming initiative is to participate in the kind
> of love that God gives regularly: as God gives sunshine
> and rain to enemies as well as friends, so are we to give
> love and prayers to our enemies as well as our friends. I
> could hardly be clearer that the transforming initiative

is participative in God's active presence and God's grace. In practicing this kind of love, we are "children of our Father in heaven". [22]

God's "Extra Mile" Mercy Plan

The word "blessed" means congratulations, an ascription of blessing, to be happy, and experiencing joy regardless of the situation. We find an underlying happiness for the person who is willing to put these eight Beatitudes into daily practice. Blessed are you when you show mercy, make peace, are persecuted for the sake of righteousness, and are poor in spirit. All of these lessons are to help us to become the boaters and swimmers who know that, with Jesus guiding our lives, we will make it safely to the other side. The fear of drowning even in the deepest of waters has been rectified. Thank God for His mercy!

In *What Did Jesus Mean?* Anna Wierzbicka states that mercy is more than merely not responding in anger—it is repaying evil with good:

> The image of turning the other cheek implies not only the absence of any retaliation or revenge but also an active message of non-retaliation: a message that sets the scene for subsequent images, which take us further still. It is not enough to repay the attacker in kind, it is not enough to give up retaliation altogether, and it is not enough to convey one's complete lack of bad intentions, one should go so far as to repay evil with good, that is to do (or want to do) something good for the "evil person". [23]

Mercy has "the outward action of a manifestation of pity and assumes need on the part of him who receives". [24] The merciful are those who extend to people around them, who touch the lives of others with the incredible action of mercy—even when retaliation is called for. The book of Isaiah captures the mercy of God in this passage that reads, *"Come let us reason together says the Lord. Though your sins are like scarlet they shall be white as snow. Though they are red as crimson they shall be like wool"* (Isaiah 1:18).

Mercy, as extended by God, is the greatest motivator for the believer to live a merciful life. Mercy means that you have adequate resources to meet the needs of the one who requires the action. Jesus will not allow us to extend mercy only to the deserving, but when the law might require action against another, mercy should be extended with grace and goodness.

If we were to receive a bill for one thousand dollars to be paid upon opening, and we have two thousand dollars in our checking account, we are able to meet the need. Many companies will extend grace to us through what they term a "grace period", which gives us a little more time to cover the debt. If we do not have the resources to cover the incurred debt, then mercy could be extended through "debt forgiveness" to cover our inability to pay. There are also times when the Law requires punishment, where the mercy of the court can be petitioned to extend a gracious probation.

When we throw ourselves upon God's mercy, He is more than able to cover our debt. God, who is rich in mercy, has adequate resources to cover any action or debt requiring forgiveness.

Lloyd-Jones speaks to us of meeting God and the cost of forgiveness:

> The Christian is a man who believes he is going to look into the face of Christ. And when that great morning comes, when he looks into the face of One who endured the cruel cross for him in spite of his vileness, he does not want to remember, as he looks into those eyes, that he refused to forgive someone while he was here on earth, or that he did not love that other person, but despised and hated him and did everything he could against him.
>
> [25]

Reputation and Retaliation

You have heard that it was said, 'Eye for eye and tooth for tooth.' But I tell you, do not resist an evil person. If someone strikes you on the right cheek, turn to him the other also. Matthew 5:38-39

Mercy is given to limit a response—not to use in response toward someone else or by "evil means." In Kingdom Ethics, the authors note:

> In a seldom-noticed insight, Clarence Jordon has pointed out that the Greek for "evil" can mean either "by evil means or "the evil person". Either translation is equally good according to Greek grammar; the decision must come from the context. The context is that Jesus repeatedly confronts evil, but never by evil means, and never by means of revengeful violence. Therefore, the context favors the instrumental "do not resist by evil means". [26]

If one cow was stolen, you could not respond by taking five cows from the offender. The response was intended to limit the retaliation against the one who was wronged. Carson also states the value and purpose of the Law:

> The Jewish people had heard that it was said, "An eye for an eye and a tooth for a tooth." This famous law is found in Exodus 21, Leviticus 24, and Deuteronomy 19. First, however prescriptive it might have been, it was also restrictive, and therefore it was an excellent tool for eliminating blood feuds and intertribal warfare. [27]

Everything within us desires to be vindicated. Vengeance has found its way into most of people's dealings with each other, from financial scandals to immoral affairs and lost opportunities. Grace extended to the unworthy is more than an idea, it is a prescription for those whom Jesus addresses. He is speaking about reputations, retaliation, and recuperating the evil person.

The way to eliminate evil is not to retaliate against it. Jesus often addressed the religious people and problems of that day, though never with violence. Although He questioned the Pharisees, situations, interpretation of the Law, He did so nonviolently.

So, should we, as believers never respond when attacked? Such extremes would preclude Christians from joining the police force or serving in the military. This interpretation would cheapen the words of Jesus when he tells us not to *"resist an evil person."* The belief exists that there are indeed evil people who should be resisted, and that a greater good would be accomplished in such an action.

Jesus stated in John 18:23, *"If I said something wrong, testify as to what is wrong. But if I spoke the truth, why did you strike Me?"* This is one of the moments where even the Son of God acknowledges that there are situations that should be questioned; though He would not retaliate, He questioned the very act that had taken place.

Paul stated of his offenders, *"They beat us publicly without a trial, even though we are Roman citizens, and threw us into prison. And now do they want to get rid us quietly? No! Let them come themselves and escort us out"* (Acts 16:37). The early church, under such extreme persecution, was spared further hurt by Paul's courageous words.

If someone strikes you on the cheek with an open hand, it is more demeaning to your reputation than a fighting stance. Again, Stassen and Gushee both acknowledge that the slap is not about physical discomfort, but about being insulted:

> A slap with the right hand on the right cheek would be a
> slap with the back of the hand. This would be an insult to
> someone's honor, the way you would slap a slave, saying,

"you cur," "you dog, you have no honor." To turn the other cheek is not simply to put up with the insult; it is to turn the cheek of equal dignity. [28]

There is a balance between what we should actively endure and when we should respond to protect others or ourselves. Jesus is speaking to us about how we view our place in the world when we are unfairly ridiculed.

In the past, throughout Europe as well as America, a man's face would be struck with a glove in order to challenge his honor. Many times this act would lead to a duel with swords or, later, pistols. The last man standing was declared the winner and justice was served.

Jesus not only instructs his followers to become the servants of all, He asks them to turn the other cheek for good measure. We are not to retaliate, but to expose our reputations to further insult. The context is not about protecting your family, or stopping another person from being threatened. It is the call to put yourself before others, even when it means your honor may be questioned.

Dispossessing Rights

And if someone wants to sue you and take your tunic, let him have your cloak as well. Matthew 5:40

In the United States, we believe in certain freedoms of expression. Many regard their chosen life style as a right, something owed to them. The pursuit of happiness is embraced as a goal, worthy of seeking at any cost. We have rights to cherish and protect, but if we find ourselves in an unwarranted lawsuit or experiencing friction from a neighbor, we feel our rights are being called into question.

Forgiveness, though sought after, has more to do with further humiliation than a resolved action. Who would seek their own humiliation? What about our rights? Where does mercy and forgiveness come in to play?

Humiliation enters our world at an early age through simple, inevitable experiences, like being last in line or the forgotten person in a friendly game at school. Rarely would a person choose to be humiliated.

When we feel our life is up for the taking, we begin the easily adaptable act of casting blame. We blame our past or the way our family raised us or treated us. We blame our relationships for lacking the intimacy needed to grow. We blame systems that choose personality over substance, money over love, and lawsuits over mercy.

This is why our concerns, as followers of Jesus Christ, are about other people, and never about our reputation or rights. Craig Keener expounds upon the legal ramifications of showing mercy that goes beyond what is required:

> Because the outer cloak doubled as a poor man's bedding, biblical law permitted no one to take it; even as a pledge overnight (Ex. 22:26-27; Deut. 24:12-13). Thus Jesus demands that we surrender the very possession the law explicitly protects from legal seizure (Guelich 1982:222). To force his hearers to think then, Jesus provides a shockingly graphic almost humorous illustration of what He means by nonresistance. [29]

Enlisted Service

If someone forces you to go one mile, go with him two miles. Give to the one who asks you, and do not turn away from the one who wants to borrow from you. Matthew 5:41-42

Life is filled with inopportune incidents that take us out of our routine. The phone may ring from a friend who needs a ride to the airport in twenty minutes, disrupting our plans. Or, perhaps you come across someone standing at a traffic light asking for financial help when you are unsure of their truthfulness. Do we help all who ask? Should we give, even when it puts our own things at risk? We try to stay uninvolved, even though many choices face us each day that cry for mercy. Whistling in the dark will no more exorcise evil than avoiding the needs of others will cause them to disappear. We must allow others to take precedence over our private agendas and personal rights.

One day, I was up at the lake where we keep our boat. I was wearing a T-shirt—with a Coke logo written in Hebrew on the front—which I had bought weeks before in Israel. I was busy shopping in town for a few things when a young man came up to me speaking in Hebrew! He had seen the shirt and thought I was Israeli. My hands were full, I was in a hurry, and the young man—here for military training—was looking for a friendly face. I set aside my plans and took him and his wife on a trip around the lake. He was grateful and a quick study, and in those few moments together, we built bridges between two countries. Mercy has many choices, including learning to listen when your agenda seems full. You may have to go the extra mile—or in the case that day—an extra tour around the lake.

The merciful understand that there is always greater reward in the giving than in receiving. In going one mile, you may find yourself doubling the requirement. Society's implicit rules are being used more as a measuring gauge than as a way of life. Have I fulfilled all of my requirements? Willard explains the simple truth of nonresistance:

> "Go with him two" (Matthew 5:41). If a policeman or other responsible official exercises a right to require assistance from them, they will do more than is strictly required of them, as an expression of their goodwill toward the official and his or her responsibility. They will have regard to the person involved and act from the kingdom on their behalf. They will consider the problem of the official to be something of importance to themselves. [30]

The value of acknowledging another's needs before your own is the very foundation of this Beatitude. Paul states clearly, *"He who has been stealing must steal no longer, but must work, doing something useful with his own hands, that he may have something to share with those in need"* (Ephesians 4:28). It is that simple. The merciful are responsible to go the extra mile, to give to those who ask to borrow. It is not our place to judge, nor our responsibility to determine if what is given or done will be for the deserving. Being enlisted for God's service is about our hearts.

Elijah, after years of no rain, asked the widow to give him something to eat. Her response was direct and clear—she did not have enough for even one more meal to feed herself and her son. The prophet declared that if he ate, she would not run out of flour or oil until the day it rained. Her faith was an example of trusting God and giving when it seemed a fruitless action. (See 1 Kings 17:17-26.)

Service is always a part of the disciple's job description. What if, as believers, we carried towels as our identifiers? As Jesus wrapped himself with a towel and washed the disciples' feet, we should "wash the feet" of those we serve by going further and giving more. In the book *Kingdom Ethics*, the language of being compelled is the embrace of the cross:

> And the Greek word for that means "forces" or "compels" in the phrase "if someone compels you to go one mile," is the same word used when Simon of Cyrene is compelled to carry Jesus' cross, thus participating in Jesus' crucifixion with Him (Matthew 27:32). Jesus gave his life for us. When we go the second mile as an initiative of peacemaking, when we give to the poor, we are participating in the way of Jesus who was crucified for us. We are participating in the grace of the cross. [31]

When we put others first, the example of Christ is clearly seen and experienced. Though life is full of situations that we cannot control, the merciful always find ways to extend grace beyond expectations.

Perfection in You

You have heard that it was said, "Love your neighbor" and hate your enemy. But I tell you: Love your enemies and pray for those who persecute you, that you may be sons of your Father in heaven. He causes His sun to rise on the evil and the good, and sends rain on the righteous and the unrighteous. If you love those who love you, what reward will you get? Are not even the tax collectors doing that? And if you greet only your brothers, what are you doing more than others? Do not even pagans do that? Be perfect, therefore, as your heavenly Father is perfect. Matthew 5:43-48

We are blessed when we show mercy, especially when it is to those with whom we did not have a prior relationship. By what we extend to others, we in turn receive. Forgive and you will be forgiven. Give and it will be given back to you. Lose your life and you will find it.

Perfection in you will happen by divine appointment and will find its work through your very enemies. God is far more concerned about what He is doing in you than by what will be accomplished through you.

The phrase, *"You have heard it said"*, always introduces a new application of Jesus's teaching with a different, usually unexpected action. An idea may have been interpreted by tradition and culture one way, but now Jesus will offer much-needed clarification. "Love your enemies"—as quoted by John Piper—remains the true test of a disciple:

> The injunction to "love your enemies" is generally regarded as the heart of Jesus' teaching, and nobody doubts either its authenticity or its centrality. To quote Piper's (1979:1) book, which has these words as its title, "Love your enemies!" is one of the few sayings of Jesus

the authenticity of which is not seriously questioned by anyone. Nor is it disputed that this command is crucial in understanding what the earthly Jesus wanted to accomplish. [32]

In these words, Jesus asks for what would seem pure fantasy. Pray for your enemies. Give up your reputation. Do not retaliate. Go the extra mile and give to those who ask. This teaching is profound and seemingly impossible to fulfill; however, there is hope! The floodwaters in Genesis rose twenty feet above the highest mountain; people drowned—except those saved through obedience in building the ark. Anything we are required to perfect for others is not a burden—but a blessing—for these lessons keep us swimming on top of the water and prevent us from drowning. Here, Carson explains that this teaching embraces the character of God:

> After all, God "causes His sun to rise on the evil and the good, and send rain on the righteous and the unrighteous" (Matthew 5:45). God loved rebellious sinners so much He sent his Son (John 3:16; Romans 5:8); and, if we are His sons, we will have his character. To be persecuted because of righteousness is to align oneself with the prophets (Matthew 5:12); but to bless and pray for those who persecute us to align oneself with the character of God. [33]

The concluding remarks of the passage make this demand: the impossible call to be perfect.

> "Perfect means designed for a specific purpose; complete, conveying the idea of that which is good, perfect." [34]

This idea of perfection was created for a certain reason, for a particular use. Perfection refers to being like God (perfect, lacking nothing), thus fulfilling the reason we were created. Each of us has different gifts and different callings. Each of us cannot escape the need to become like Christ. Lloyd-Jones reminds us of this very truth:

> The Christian is essentially a unique and special kind of person. This is something which can never be emphasized sufficiently. There is nothing more tragic than the failure on the part of many professing Christians to realize the uniqueness and the special character of a Christian. He [sic] is a man [sic] who can never be explained in natural terms...a man [sic] who is doing more than others; he does what others cannot do. [35]

I think a perfect day for me and my family could be described as heading to the lake—finding the water is like glass, the weather beautiful and warm, and our boat starting and in good running order—everything we are looking for happens, fitting perfectly into our experience.

When humanity finds the reason we were created, the exact place in which we can fulfill our calling in Christ, we realize this is a perfect life. Not that life is without its storms, but we realize we have accomplished what God has asked us to do each day. Perfection is about striving, swimming, pressing every day to become the extraordinary people the Father has desired for us to be.

Perfection can also mean, "to tighten" until the object or person has reached a level of acceptable limits. The carpenter who hangs a door will not say the job is complete until the screws are tightened without being stripped. The mechanic working on a car engine knows there are specifications for how tight certain bolts must be kept. The wheels on a car must have a certain torque to remain tight. The bolt that carries the exact specifications it was designed for, when tightened, is then declared perfect.

God is not in the business of "stripping" anyone, but He will tighten us spiritually each day so that we continue to become a perfect example of a growing disciple. Swimming—though never perfected—becomes so much a part of our lives that we find it easier to stay in the race and finish the course set out before us.

When my children were born, they were perfect in my estimation. The book of James relates, *"Every good and perfect gift is from above, coming down from the Father of the heavenly lights, who does not change like shifting shadows. He chose to give us birth through the word of truth, that we might be a kind of first-fruits of all He created"* (James 1:17-8). Though they could not talk, walk, or even smile, they were perfect as created. Over the next months, they changed in size and expectations. We loved them at every age and stage of life; though they were in our eyes perfect, we expected growth. Over time, they developed their speech, started walking, and remained perfect in many ways.

Our heavenly Father does not lavish His love upon us after we have proven our faithfulness. He loves us, and extends that love even to those who do not acknowledge Him. Perfection also carries a sense of striving and accomplishment. In his second letter to the Corinthians, Paul encourages this as a goal, *"Finally, brothers, good-bye. Aim for perfection, listen to my appeal, be of one mind; live in peace. And the God of love and peace will be with you"* (2 Corinthians 13:11).

Though we saw our children in different stages as perfect, we were not satisfied. They could crawl but we were waiting for their first steps. They could say, "Da-Ma," but we were waiting for "Daddy" or "Mommy." As they grew, we anticipated their personal growth.

Perfection should not be understood as a burdensome impossibility from an unyielding father, but as a loving directive as a daily activity of mercy shown to others, as received from our heavenly Father.

A Perfect Day

Praise the Lord, O my soul, and forget not all His benefits—who forgives all your sins and heals all your diseases... Psalm 103:2-3

The merciful know that life will be filled with moments where your boat is about to sink from the waves—possibly even caused by another boater—and that forgiveness must be extended. The merciful know that no matter how well you can swim, you will drown without the help of Jesus. In His grace we have been kept from death and brought into His rich mercy. We are not only to show mercy, but also to go the extra mile, forgiving, borrowing, and serving.

The extraordinary life exemplified in following Christ is one that will be "blessed". Perfection will not be self-accomplished, or earned through some merit system. We are all in need of a Savior and through Christ we find our relationship to God restored. In following Christ, what would seem impossible is declared perfect.

The day that my daughter and I almost died in the boating accident was about more than just the loss of our boat—it was a real test of mercy. The boater who hit us was borrowing the boat from his company and was insured through a large distributor of boating parts. Because boats have no seat belts, you can claim just about any injury and no one can refute it.

I was told that we could have made a real case for a lawsuit. Instead, we had a few visits to the chiropractor and released the party at fault of any liability.

Mercy, going the extra mile, letting your face be slapped twice, is about giving when you could take. What a different church, country, and world would it be if we were willing to show mercy and constraint, when our reputations or rights were called into question?

God had kept us from drowning that day, of that I am sure. Mercy that was extended to us was in turn extended to those who had caused the damage. The merciful receive what others cannot give—the peace of knowing that you have lived what God would call a perfect day.

The Problem of Eating and Swimming

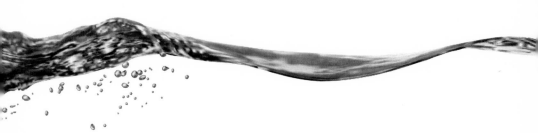

Blessed are those who hunger and thirst for righteousness,
for they shall be filled. Matthew 5:6

Explanation: Matthew 6:1-18

All of my life, I have heard that after eating, one should not swim until at least an hour has passed. Rest assured that when we were younger, none of us heeded that warning for one second. The rule had something to do with stomach cramps, but I seem to remember studies showing that it really did not make much of a difference either way—waiting after eating or jumping right in.

Jesus will establish in this Beatitude a completely different "heads up" for His followers in the water. Swimmers who desire to finish the race without drowning will need the right kind of food. Satisfaction will come to those who understand that it is possible to hunger for the right truth, which will nourish the most depleted of swimmers.

We spent so many weekends at swimming events that it became second nature to have the smell of chlorine in our cars. At almost every event, our daughter would tell me and my wife that she was starving. The diet she subsisted on would have made any other mere mortal obese, but the calories burned at a swimming event were in the thousands. We were dumbfounded as our daughter and her teammates would down a pizza, hamburgers, and a chocolate shake, then jump in the water to swim 1000 yards. I would have thoughts about sinking to the bottom with that kind of food in my stomach. Though for her, the real hunger was not during the meets, but immediately following. We even had to make emergency stops at the first fast food outlet, or our daughter just knew she would faint if we traveled one more mile. She was so hungry that a birthright could be bought for chicken tenders! While swimming, she had depleted all her energy and needed nourishment that would help her regain what she had lost.

This kind of hunger can be overwhelming and all encompassing. When you get to that stage, you can think of nothing else. Hunger cannot be satisfied by fast food alone, and true hunger for God will only be fulfilled through passionate thirsting for righteousness. What keeps you hungering after God is the belief that everything stems from and through our relationship to God and His church. Bill Hybels believes there is only one hope for mankind:

> Businessmen can provide sorely needed jobs. Wise educators can teach useful knowledge of the world. Self-help programs can offer effective methods of behavior modification. Advanced psychological techniques can aid self-understanding. And all of this is good. But can any of it truly transform the human heart? I believe that

only one power exists on this sorry planet that can do that. It's the power of the love of Jesus Christ, the love that conquers sin and wipes out shame and heals wounds and reconciles enemies and patches broken dreams and ultimately changes the world, one life at a time. And what grips my hearts every day is the knowledge that the radical message of that transforming love has been given to the church. [36]

A Righteous Appetite

Blessed are those who hunger and thirst for righteousness, for they shall be filled. Matthew 5:6

This Beatitude challenges us to walk the path that integrity has set. The definition of righteousness is right choice, or just action.

While growing up, I found it was easy to eat chips and drink cola and when it was time for the main meal, I was not hungry. "You'll spoil your dinner" was the ultimate warning against snacking on junk food. Hunger for righteousness cannot be satisfied with the junk food of poor choices. Living out the Beatitudes is restricted to what will bring the greatest fulfillment.

There are two types of righteousness—one being the righteousness of God. Paul stated, *"But now a righteousness from God apart from law, has been made known to which the law and the prophets testify. This righteousness from God comes through faith in Jesus Christ to all who believe"* (Romans 3:21-22). This first type of righteousness is the lifeline to the drowning swimmer. We will never acquire this type of righteousness except through faith. The actions of Christ caused all of creation to witness God reaching down to save the lost and sinking.

The second righteousness is a Godlike righteousness. Again Paul explains, *"And to put on the new self created to be like God in true righteousness and holiness"* (Ephesians 4:24). Therefore, we accept God's righteousness through faith and change ourselves each day by putting into practice these righteous actions. Our righteous acts begin with a changed heart and a renewed mind. Until we hunger and thirst for this kind righteousness, we will not see true and lasting change.

We are saved by faith, but the application of these lessons teaches us to swim. Blessed are those who put into practice giving, praying, and fasting as personal disciplines that will keep us from filling up on cheap grace. There is no better definition of cheap grace than that offered by Dietrich Bonhoeffer:

> Cheap grace is the preaching of forgiveness without requiring repentance, baptism without church discipline, communion without confession, absolution without personal confession. Cheap grace is grace without discipleship, grace without the cross; grace without Jesus Christ, living and incarnate. Costly grace is the treasure hidden in the field; for the sake of it a man will gladly go and sell all that he has. It is the pearl of great price to buy that which the merchant will sell all his goods for. It is the kingly rule of Christ, for whose sake a man will pluck out the eye which causes him to stumble, it is the call of Jesus Christ at which the disciple leaves his nets and follows Him. [37]

A Right Reward

Be careful not do your "acts of righteousness" before men, to be seen by them. If you do, you will have no reward from your Father in heaven. So when you give to the needy do not announce it with trumpets, as the hypocrites do in the synagogues and on the streets to be honored by men. Matthew 6:1-2

Jesus, too, warns, *"Be careful not to do your 'acts of righteousness' before men"* (Matthew 6:1). You will find warning signs at any public beach or lake where there is no lifeguard on duty. "Swim at your own risk" is posted, often with flashing lights to remind eager swimmers of danger.

Today, those committed to swimming in deep waters know that only Jesus can keep us from drowning and that we must realize that our actions are being watched. Still, though we may have all the technical moves to be a qualified swimmer, we may swim for the wrong reasons—for recognition and not for God's glory. So many accomplishments may have false motives and may be undertaken for personal recognition. "Be careful" was a warning for those who were by the Sea of Galilee, and it is for those today who choose to live their lives by the same lessons.

We live in a world with excessive stuff, with the latest electronic inventions, with worldwide information available in seconds—and yet, we are the most dissatisfied people. We have innumerable books on self-help, self-awareness, and true happiness, yet these goals seem elusive. We do not find happiness in marriage, we do not find happiness in drugs, and we do not find happiness in addictive behaviors.

From the shores of Galilee, Jesus reminds us that, *"Those who will hunger and thirst for righteousness, they will be filled [satisfied]"* (Matthew 5:6). Hunger that drives us to satisfaction will only come when we are willing to trust that what God offers us is lasting. When you are really thirsty, soft drinks will not help, nor will iced tea; you want a glass of water because that is the only liquid that was made to truly satisfy our thirst. Righteousness is the only truly satisfying action.

The concept of the reward system has served in every household since childrearing began. There is a reward for cleaning up your room or a reward for doing a specific task—the reward is the reinforcement. When our daughter had her tonsils out and refused to start eating again, we had to devise a reward system. A beanie baby for each meal she ate for a few days was enough of a reward to get her eating again.

When we follow Jesus, we are rewarded with happiness, blessings, and peace. We may look forward to the reward of heaven and eternal life.

We are to live in this world being salt and light, yet never for recognition. Jesus addressed the gathering in order to spread the truth of the earned reward as a wage or a payment. This reward can be paid in full or in deferred installments. The reward that you seek from the Father is a reward that is paid in secret. Those who realize that they will drown without being rescued by Christ, act so that they will reap rewards lasting well beyond this lifetime.

Three words may be found to describe the actions in a stage production. Hypocrite is the same word for being on stage as a character or actor. The second word—seen—asks the hearer not to be motivated by self-recognition. Lastly, the concept of the reward may relate to how a stage production ends with the customary applause. Craig Keener writes about how leaders need to remember they are not hired actors for pay, but people living for service to God:

> Yet the same temptation is no less real today. Jesus reminds us that true piety means impressing God alone—living our lives in the approval alone that matters. Mathew again praises the meek, whose only hope is in God, not in others' opinions of them. Those of us who are "religious professionals," making our living from public ministry, should take special heed: if we value the approval or pay of our congregations more than what God has called us to do, we will have no reward left when we stand before Him. [38]

The Greeks loved to stage plays and the vibrant culture soon spread all the way to Rome. They built theaters and amphitheaters in every Roman city to feature their elaborately staged productions.

Jesus tells us that if we are going to be actors on the stage of life, then we will receive an actor's reward. The reward for acting is man's applause and the reward is paid in full. After the performance, the actor must find another show, another stage in order to receive another reward. When the applause has faded away you have already received your reward in full. The actors, or hypocrites, put on masks, becoming other people for the production.

Henri Nouwen captures the essence of the temptation even for Jesus to be popular:

> The second temptation to which Jesus was exposed was precisely the temptation to do something spectacular, something that could win him great applause. *"Throw yourself from the parapet of the temple and let the angels catch you and carry you in their arms" (Matthew 4:6). But Jesus refused to be a stunt man. He did not come to prove himself. He did not come to walk on hot coals, swallow fire, or put His hand in the lion's mouth to demonstrate that he had something worthwhile to say. "Don't put the Lord your God to the test,"* He said. [39]

We are all hypocrites in some way or another, but Jesus will not allow us to think we are different. Even key leaders and righteous-seeming individuals are receiving their rewards in full. Jesus is concerned that we seek the true reward, which is paid in secret.

The book of Genesis states, *"Fear not, Abraham. I am your shield and your very great reward"* (Genesis 15:1). The Psalmist declares, *"Keep the word of the Lord, in them is great reward"* (Psalm 19:4). Again we see, *"Surely the righteous will be rewarded"* (Psalm 58:11). John records the words of Jesus in the book of Revelation, *"Behold I am coming soon and My reward is with Me"* (Revelation 22:12).

We must make sure the reward that we seek is eternal; otherwise what we are receiving is only transitory appreciation. The need to be seen, acknowledged, and appreciated can rob the individual of the act of service. In the book *A New Kind of Christian*, the author captures the belief of an emerging generation that cries for genuine followers of Christ to live differently:

> By monastery, I would want the seminarians to live in community of some sort, to experience a real sharing of life and of "the offices" of shared spiritual practices. This would contribute to spiritual formation and it would weed out sociopathic types who are attracted to ministry because they like power or they like being right or they need attention but they don't love or serve people much. [40]

The Reward of Giving

So when you give to the needy, do not announce it with trumpets, as the hypocrites do in the synagogues and on the streets, to be honored by men. I tell you they have received their reward in full. But when you give to the needy, do not let your left hand know what your right is doing, so that your giving may be in secret. Then your Father, who sees what is done in secret, will reward you. Matthew 6:2-4

This kind of giving that Jesus talks about is, in fact, an act of personal recognition—like tooting your own horn, so to speak. Trumpets of self-praise, baskets of self-attention, and hands of self-proclamation are three specific areas of service that Jesus deals with in giving. Few people desire to hear instructions about giving. There has been national attention on abuses in giving and finances from banks to investors calling for a new relationship with the Father.

We can drive a boat, but we can find ourselves in storms where we are no longer in control—even with the best navigation. All that we have is in God's hands and we are learning how to give righteously without it ever being seen. Giving is one of the disciplines that reminds us we are not in control. Pride makes us desire recognition when we give. God is not asking us if we want to give, He tells us that the world is His and that He is going to require us to give as we have received.

The Old Testament calls Israel the "Promised Land" and that title never changes. What is promised always remains in God's ultimate control. In our acts of giving, we must be ever mindful of being ensnared in the desire to be seen and applauded. We are to live as disciples of Christ, to be His hands for no other purpose than to bring glory to God.

Many times people would have trumpets blown when they entered into the synagogue—and they then received their reward in full. The more money they put into the offering, the louder the trumpets, and the greater the applause. However, Jesus observed a widow who put two small copper coins in the offering, and in seeing this act, He declared that she gave the greatest of all amounts—all that she had (Luke 21:1-4). Again, Lloyd-Jones offers insight into seeking the right reward:

> When we truly come to examine our hearts we find that there are very subtle ways in which this self-same thing can be done. Well, that is the wrong way and the result of that is this: 'Verily I say unto you, they have their reward. People praise and say, "how wonderful, how marvelous; terrific, isn't it?" They get their reward, they get their praise. They get their names in the paper; articles are written about them; there is a great deal of talk about them; people write their obituary notices; they get it all. Poor men that is all they will get; they will get nothing from God. [41]

We are encouraged to notice even the smallest expression of pride in giving. Our hands are used to place our money into the offering plates—or, in that day, receptacles. The opportunity for recognition can even be found in how we use our hands. Today, many churches use the "offering envelope" for privacy and ease of record keeping. If we have an offering, and we pass the monetary gift from one hand to the other for people to see, we have our reward in full. Not allowing one hand to know what the other is doing curtails any attempt to draw attention to our gift as we place it in the offering. Shifting the gift from one hand to the other allows people to glimpse our offering, and many receive recognition, or applause, for the amount given. We have our reward in full.

Acts of righteousness have, unfortunately, digressed into monetary gifts. Alms, as they are known, can be an act of righteousness, of helping a neighbor in need. Acts of righteousness can be giving food to the hungry, caring for the sick, or reaching out to the poor. Those are acts of righteousness that only the Father knows and rewards. The reward we should seek does not come from others but from God in His time.

May mankind see us glorifying God with our lives, serving each other in love without the need to be rewarded by anyone but the Father, who repays in secret.

The Reward of Prayers

And when you pray, do not be like the hypocrites, for they love to pray standing in the synagogues and on the street corners to be seen by men. I tell you the truth; they have received their reward in full. But when you pray, go into your room, close the door and pray to your Father who sees what is done in secret, will reward you. And when you pray, do not keep babbling like pagans, for they think they will be heard because of their many words. Do not be like them, for your Father knows what you need before you ask him. This then is how you should pray: "Our Father in heaven, hallowed be Your name, Your kingdom come, Your will be done, on earth as it is in heaven. Give us today our daily bread. Forgive us our debts, as we also have forgiven our debtors. And lead us not into temptation but deliver us from the evil one." For if you forgive men, when they sin against you, your heavenly Father will also forgive you. But if you do not forgive men their sins, your Father will not forgive you your sins. Matthew 6:5-15

Prayer is a righteous act and a necessary part of any lesson. It is one of the acts of righteousness in the life of the disciple that is rewarded by the Father, who wants us to hunger for nothing else. Much has been written about the power of entering into prayer. Eugene Peterson reminds us of the awesome power of prayer:

> Prayer is a daring venture into speech that juxtaposes our words with the sharply alive words that pierce and divide souls and spirit, joints and marrow, pitilessly exposing every thought and intention of the heart (Hebrews 4:12-13; Revelation 1:16). If we had kept our mouths shut we would not have involved ourselves in such a relentlessly fearsome exposure. If we had been content to speak to the women and men and children in the neighborhood we could have gotten by with using words in ways that would have them thinking well of us while concealing what we preferred to keep to ourselves. But when we venture into prayer, every word may, at any moment, come to mean just what it means and involve us with a holy God who wills our holiness. [42]

The Living God inhabits the praise of His people, and we will be truly satisfied when prayer becomes the instrument for channeling that power into our lives and the lives of those for whom we intercede. However, Jesus teaches us that even our prayers can be corrupted and used for self-recognition.

Leaders, disciples, and fellow swimmers following Christ must find the central discipline of prayer to be equal to breathing. Good swimmers will find that bringing their heads out of the water to breathe is awkward and costly in time, as well as in energy. Keeping your head down in the water while swimming and turning it to the side for a breath can increase your effectiveness and grace in the water.

Prayer is not meant to be awkward, nor is it to bring attention to you. It is as simple as taking a breath while continuing to press ahead in your calling. Prayer—true communion with God—can become the ballast in a stormy world.

Answered prayer is one of the "signs" that Jesus works through our lives to manifest His Glory. God seems to be more ready to answer than we are to ask. We are asked again to "be careful"—taking to heart the admonition and praying with full exposure and not hiding behind a mask of religious recognition.

We are to live as servants, forgive as forgiven, and pray so that the Father can repay in secret. When you pray, find a room that is closed off from others, a hidden place where none but the Father knows what you are asking with careful purpose and selflessness.

Sometimes a prayer closet is your car; sometimes it's an office when nobody is around. These are the times that the Father knows that you are crying out to Him. Paul reminds us to *"pray continually"* (1 Thessalonians 5:17). Those who hunger and thirst for righteousness will pursue a prayerful life that does not focus on themselves or on what others are thinking.

I have witnessed church services in which prayer requests have turned into opportunities to gossip about another person. The actions can be subtle, but ultimately reveal that our hearts are not turned towards the righteousness that will satisfy. When God hears us and responds with His reward, we find peace that goes beyond anything that people can recognize.

The warning to be careful is followed by an example of prayer that the Father seeks. We do not need to babble and repeat the same words over and over again to impress others with how long we can pray. Prayer is like holding our breath under water. It does not matter how long we can hold our breath—eventually we will all need air. Prayer is not measured by the length or the number of words, but by heart and faith. Prayers that closed the mouths of lions or called down fire on a sacrifice were mere seconds in length. Somebody could pray for 15 minutes with good diction and great enunciation, yet God still hears the sinner who cries out, "I need help."

Jesus declares, *"This, then, is how you should pray"* (Matthew 6:9). He did not state that this prayer would be a mantra that we could quote, but a clear counter-expression to the hypocrite's long vocal performances. In the book, *Lord, Teach Us: The Lord's Prayer & the Christian Life*, we see how this prayer is a testimony that we are His disciples:

> By learning to pray the Lord's Prayer, we do not become better than other people—at least in the sense that "better" is used in our society. We do not become better; we become Christian. That is, we become disciples of Jesus who have no need to claim that we are better than other people since our prayer now is a witness to what God has done among ordinary sinful folk like us by teaching us how to pray. [43]

The Lord's Prayer—as it is commonly referred to—settles our relationship as disciples in the discipline of prayer. *"Our Father who is in heaven"* (Matthew 6:9) settles our relationship to the Father. He is our Father and offers us a heavenly perspective as a model.

"Your kingdom come, your will be done on earth as it is in heaven" (Matthew 6:10) settles the place of God's kingdom in our lives. Leadership is always formed when we come under the rulership of God's kingdom.

We, who have no delusion that we were drowning without Christ, now understand the kingdom of God and choose to submit ourselves daily. We are asked to submit our very thoughts to God's Kingdom through prayer. Willard reminds us of the value of thinking:

> Paying careful attention to how Jesus made use of logical thinking can strengthen our confidence in Jesus as master of the centers of intellect and creativity and can

encourage us to accept Him as master in all of the areas of intellectual life in which we may participate. [44]

"Give us today our daily bread" (Matthew 6:11) settles our dependence on God alone. You cannot be dependent on what happened yesterday—we need bread for today. "God, I need you this day" is a prayer that speaks of the spiritual hunger that becomes a way of life.

"Forgive us our debts, as we have also have forgiven our debtors" (Matthew 6:12) settles our relationships with each other. Living in forgiveness will free us to give away what has been given to us freely through God's grace. Acts of righteousness are about the Father's recognition of how we pray and relate to the community in which God has placed us.

"And lead us not into temptation but deliver us from the evil one" (Matthew 6:13) settles our purpose in following God. There is an enemy who desires to *"rob, steal, and destroy"* (John 10:10), but Christ came to give us abundant life. Jesus settles the fact that evil [beings] exist; we can now be directed to a path in which temptation can be more easily identified.

Storms will come—we now have the grace to ask God to keep us afloat.

The Reward of Fasting

When you fast, do not look somber as the hypocrites do, for they disfigure their faces to show men they are fasting. I tell you the truth; they have received their reward in full. But when you fast, put oil on your head and wash your face so that it will not be obvious to men that you are fasting, but only to your Father who is unseen; and your Father, who sees what is done in secret, will reward you. Matthew 6:16-18

One last act of righteousness to be careful about is fasting—the combined action of our personal lives and spiritual lives. There are many types of fasts, all of which are more than dieting.

The spiritual discipline of fasting has long been the true disciple's food and the lifeline to keep us from drifting in any storm. Throughout His teachings in the gospels, Jesus mentions the practice of fasting. Forty days of prayer and fasting marked His confrontation with Satan wrestling with the temptations of recognition, power, and the very Word of God.

We are advised that some things do not happen without fasting and prayer. From the people of the Exodus, to the Assyrians of Jonah, to Esther's three-day fast before asking for her people to be spared, fasting remains to this day the discipline that leaders love to hate. The greatest hypocrite can speak of fasting as a way of life, and yet never engage in the practice from the heart. With only the desire to be recognized and applauded as one who fasts, they have their reward in full. The opposite act is to fast only for recognition from our Father.

The disciple may engage in several types of fasting. One option is a partial fast, as when Daniel ate vegetables instead of the rich food that Babylon offered. There is also another partial fast that takes place over a three-day period, as Amos and Ezra enacted. There were also forty-day fasts that were only undertaken as directed by God.

Fasting without prayer is really just dieting. The generation that seeks to engage the Father in acts of righteousness—such as fasting—seeks the heart of God. Fast with a smile, washed and dressed, so that only the Father knows what you are seeking of Him.

The Reward that Satisfies

Jesus said, *"Don't be like the hypocrites"* (Matthew 6:16), who put on their masks and parade in the streets and synagogues desiring recognition. Giving or praying or fasting are acts of righteousness only satisfying when carried out by disciples' hungering after God. Mankind's recognition and applause will die out with our reward in full. The true reward is beyond momentary recognition and held in trust by the Father who watches in secret.

There is no real prayer without forgiveness of those who have trespassed against us. Our first instinct is self-recognition, but when we are drowning, Jesus pulls us from the water into His boat. All others deserve the same from us.

Anyone who has had a boat for very long has broken down on some waterway and needed assistance. Frustration arises when boats go by while we yell and wave, yet they do not even slow down. When a battery will not turn the motor over or an unexplained electrical problem arises, we may be in a very remote area. Many times, when we lose control over the boat's direction, we are headed toward rocks and obstacles that we have no power to avoid. Boaters that happen by and throw us a line to pull us back to the dock are a very welcome help. Many times we have offered money to those who have helped us in those times of crisis, but we have yet to have anyone take the gift. They all respond the same way, "I needed a tow before, and am glad to repay what others had offered me."

Whether we need to offer forgiveness, pray for daily provision, or fast for a friend, all we have has come freely. There is no greater satisfaction or blessing than to offer something freely, without recognition for the act. Towing a boat or forgiving a debt, the truth remains the same—your Father will reward you and His reward will satisfy.

LESSON SIX:

The Art of Spiritual Dog Paddling

Blessed are the meek, for they will inherit the earth. Matthew 5:5

Explanation: Matthew 6:19-34

O ne would think that as a seventeen year old, common sense would have prevailed in my life since I had just gotten out of jail for drug possession. But, at that age, I didn't have much common sense or a brain that functioned well—and I would have never guessed that just a few hours after eating Captain Crunch cereal in the morning, I would encounter a situation where I could have found myself possibly on life support in the afternoon.

I was riding in a van that day with my friends to Little Rock Dam, popularly referred to as the swimming hole where ditching high school seniors could drown. The water was very deep—at least twenty feet over our heads. My friends and I were up to the challenge of swimming across the lake, jumping off sheer cliffs, and swimming back. It did not matter that the only exercise any of us had recently had consisted of arm movements to get various substances into our mouths. We threw caution to the wind and went for the other side. We were just thirty feet from shore. So far, so good. The sun was warm, and it was a perfect day not to drown—because drowning would ruin the outing.

All of us arrived across the lake, climbed the cliffs, and jumped into the water from about thirty-feet high. We had no clue how deep the water was, and what lurked beneath seemed of little consequence. We quickly tired of climbing the cliff just for a two-second thrill. Like snow tubing, there was too much work for only a few seconds of terror. We began swimming back across—though swimming is a euphemism. We were really dog paddling, inching our way toward the shore.

In that moment, I made a personal inventory of what my parents would find if someone discovered my drowned body lying face down with a few fish and a turtle or two. How had I come to this? I muttered and sputtered a feeble prayer, something like, "God I'm drowning here," and quickly learned that floating on my back helped. I made it to the van and swore I would never be that stupid again—but, of course, stupid is a relative term.

I contemplated my demise and realized I couldn't make it on my own. My dog paddling technique almost put my life into over twenty feet of deep, dark water. Although that day was over forty years ago, I've found myself in many other situations dog paddling my way to some distant answer that would probably end in failure. Facing weakness is not for the faint of heart; it leads to false bravado and unrealized dreams, like when Old Blue Eyes sings, "I did it my way"—but now I'm paying for it. That tune has just one lyric: "Me, me, me."

The truth is that I am unable physically, emotionally, or spiritually to make it on my own without leaving a wake of desperate prayers, bad choices, and improbable undertakings.

God Saves Swimmers in Deep Water

Included in the Sermon on the Mount are eight of the greatest blessings uttered by the greatest Teacher on how not to drown while swimming in life's deep waters. Jesus is a Christian's swimming coach. Although He spoke nearly two thousand years ago, the Sermon on the Mount throws a lifeline to swimmers caught in deep waters.

I'm convinced we create illusions of security. We sometimes sail on boats without life preservers, pushing off from dock without checking the weather. We can ignore these details or accept that sailing in deep water might kill us.

Dog paddling will keep us afloat for a while, even in deep water, but we must work on our swimming technique to become truly adept. My daughter has been part aquatic animal for most of her life. I went to more weekends of meets than can be numbered just to see her swim for a few seconds. I had to plan bathroom breaks between heats or miss the race I had waited half the afternoon to see. I watched some swimmers splash water everywhere and still have the slowest times. They were exhausted and emptied half the pool during the frantic races; they were just not fast enough. Great swimmers glide with very little resistance, as though they are on top of the water, while others come in last.

The more we fight God's calling, the more we splash and show little improvement despite all the effort. I perfected the dog paddle as a way to tread deep water. I thought I was making progress, but in reality I tired quickly and was disqualified because of my form. Each competitive swimming race has specific qualifications—because one wrong kick or stroke will disqualify a swimmer. Paul speaks to the same practice: *"Therefore I do not run like a man running aimlessly; I do not fight like a man beating the air. No, I beat my body and make it my slave so that after I have preached to others, I myself will not be disqualified for the prize"* (1 Corinthians 9:26-27).

I realize I must learn the rules, practice the proper strokes, and understand that dog paddling won't work for long while in deep water. Dog paddling wasn't good when I was seventeen, and at my age now, it is increasingly counterproductive. It's funny how we can revert to the same old survival methods only to reach the same old conclusions. Christianity is a means to practice, to foster a deeper relationship with Jesus. Alister McGrath speaks to the elements as a way of life:

> "Being a Christian is not just about beliefs and values, it is about real life, in which those ideas and values are expressed and embodied in a definite way of living. The everyday life of believers is affected in certain ways by their faith." [45]

Jesus gave us eight Beatitudes with practical explanations that can equip dog paddlers with the skill to keep from drowning. He also gave detailed swimming instructions through the Beatitudes in Sermon on the Mount.

The Other Side of Meekness

"Blessed are the meek for they will inherit the earth." Matthew 5:5

I once translated *"Blessed are the meek"* as "Happy are the wimpy." The Greek word for "meek" in Matthew 5:5 means "gentle, humble, considerate...unassuming." [46] This definition doesn't suggest being mild or deficient in spirit, as we use the word today.

"The meek shall inherit the earth" is a powerful statement without timid connotations. It parallels Psalm 37:11: *"The meek shall inherit the*

land and delight themselves in abundant prosperity." They do not sound like pushovers to me. W.E. Vine says of meekness:

> "It must be clearly understood, therefore, that the meekness manifested by the Lord and commended to the believer is the fruit of power. The common assumption is that when a man [sic] is meek it is because he cannot help himself; but the Lord was 'meek' because he has the infinite resources of God at His command." [47]

Christian meekness is not being wimpy; it is a life under God's control. We can be gentle, humble, considerate, and unassuming because we know God is in control. We can relax in His strength and avoid harsh, proud, inconsiderate, and pretentious behaviors.

Life under God's control is the ability to live, make decisions, transcend dog paddling, and swim effectively in life's deep waters. When you think you might drown, you can swim with God's help. In Laurel and Hardy, Stan often shifted responsibility to Ollie: "Here is another fine mess you've gotten me into." Christians can take responsibility, seek Jesus' help, follow His instruction, and swim effectively. Christian meekness is a controlled life that inherits the earth.

We sometimes find ourselves unable to dog paddle out of deep waters. Jesus calls out, "Going my way?" and offers us a seat in His boat. Dogs continue paddling after they are picked up out of the water—and it takes me time to realize I can stop struggling, too. Jesus lifted me into His rest, and I have no fear of drowning. Life can be under God's control, however, drowning is a certainty without having a personal relationship with Jesus.

When I relinquish my splashing ways to God's control, deep waters don't scare me, and meekness begins. The writer of 1 Peter 2:9 says, *"You are a chosen generation, a royal priesthood."* The writer, reminding readers who they are through God's actions and grace, continues: *"Who has called you out of darkness and into His marvelous light."* God calls us into His light.

Paul writes, *"You are God's workmanship"* (Ephesians 2:10). Our identity is created in Christ Jesus and by doing the works of God. The call gives us meaning and identity. Christian meekness results from learning and being under God's control. Donald Hagner says,

> "In view are not persons who are submissive, mild, and unassertive, but those who are humble in the sense of being oppressed (hence 'have been humbled') bent over by the injustice of the ungodly, but who are soon to be delivered." [48]

This spiritual exercise is not low-impact, but a radical change. The Sermon on the Mount reminds us—blessed are we, happy are we, and congratulated are we—when we understand what God created us to be. A blessed Christian can swim well even in deep waters.

Meekness means to come under God's control, to come under His direction, to be submitted to His leadership. Lloyd-Jones writes that the meek are under another's control:

> "Blessed are the meek," not those who trust to their own powers and abilities and their own institutions. Rather it is the very reverse of that. And this is true, not only here, but in the whole message of the Bible. You get it in that perfect story of Gideon, where God went on reducing the numbers, not adding to them. That is the spiritual method, and here it is once more emphasized in this amazing statement in the Sermon on the Mount. [49]

Meekness can be associated with animals to describe how the animal is under human control—the animal has strength, but has been humbled.

The writer of James states, *"When we put bits into the mouths of horses to make them obey us, we can turn the whole animal"* (James 3:3).

I traveled in Africa for over thirty years, and I experienced animals under human control and out of control. For example, a guide and I crept slowly through the bush in a national reserve and came upon an endangered species of rhinoceros lying on the ground. When we approached, the rhino snorted once or twice, stood up, and waited for its usual handout of hay. Ronnie the rhino was captured as a baby and raised for protection awareness. It was like a big pet, and it was so gentle we took pictures with him—horn and all. Ronnie was meek and mild, unless you forgot to bring hay.

We consider trained animals meek when they obey their trainer's commands. After a horse is broken and trained, it is considered a meek horse, although it has great power and strength and can still run great distances. Trainers consider horses valuable if they are controlled.

Scripture refers to Moses as the most humble or meekest man who ever lived. (See Numbers 12:3.) The author of the Superman stories describes Superman's alter ego, Clark Kent, as a mild-mannered reporter. Moses' and Superman's power and strength depict two ideals lived to the fullest potential. One saved a nation through his humility; the other saved the world through his strength. One parted the sea with a stick; the other leapt over tall buildings in a single bound. Look at either one and you understand that meekness is not weakness. Happy are we, blessed are we, and joyful are we when Christ controls our instincts, thoughts, and passions.

If the waters are deep and all you can do is dog paddle, it's time to start training with the champions. The Beatitudes teach about happy, joyful living in Christ when we are under His control and participate with Him in His kingdom. We depend on God for every need and bring every thought and passion under His control through Christ. A. W. Tozer captured the essence of meekness:

The meek man is not a human mouse afflicted with a sense of his own inferiority. Rather, he may be in his moral life as bold as a lion and as strong as Samson; but he has stopped being fooled about himself. He has accepted God's estimate of his own life. He knows he is weak and helpless as God has declared him to be, but paradoxically, he knows at the same time that he is in the sight of God of more importance than angels. In himself nothing; in God, everything. [50]

We can balance the right assurance policy, enlightenment, personal burdens, or "stuff" and make sense of the blessed meek.

The Right Assurance Policy

Do not store up for yourselves treasures on earth, where moth and rust destroy and where thieves break in and steal. But store up for yourselves treasures in heaven, where moth and rust do not destroy and where thieves do not break in and steal. For where your treasure is, there your heart will be also. Matthew 6:19-21

Jesus said, "...*seek first His kingdom and all His righteousness, and all these things shall be yours as well*" (Matthew 6:33). Paul states, "*I consider everything a loss*" (Philippians 3:8). The strange paradox is that we gain all when we give up all.

Our boat incurred some damage last winter. Declaring it a total loss, our insurance company paid us its full value. Our lives are covered by God's assurance policy. If we suffer a loss, we can be assured that we are covered. The cost of discipleship must be measured against what it cost Jesus to make us disciples. Swimming in deep water when you cannot touch the bottom is unnerving and frightening. We cannot tread water or dog paddle forever. Our assurance is in the paradox that the meek will inherit the earth. When the water is deep, we have confidence that Jesus will pull us from the water.

That was Peter's experience. Peter sailed in a fishing boat and Jesus came toward him while walking on the water. Peter said to Jesus, "*Tell me come to you on the water*" (Matthew 14:28). Peter, stepping out and walking toward Jesus, called out, "*Lord, save me*" (Matthew 14:30), when he became afraid and began to sink into the depths. The Scripture reports that Jesus held out His hand and pulled Peter from the deep water. Jesus is our assurance, promising the earth to the blessed meek and pulling us from the watery depths.

We moved several years ago, and we have a post office box for the first time in thirty-five years. My wife said, "A P.O. Box seems so transitory, like we are getting ready to move at any moment." Indeed, a permanent address seems more solid. We as believers receive permanent addresses in heaven because God gives us great assurance in deep waters. Christians have permanent addresses in Christ, where what matters is protected, and "*moth and rust cannot consume*" (Matthew 6:20). Only what matters will endure in the end. Water can be dangerous because people drown and metal rusts. Even the greatest of structures will eventually give way to water.

Years ago, I bought a Volkswagen bug while living in Houston, Texas. Although it was a fine example of German engineering, it was not built for southern humidity. My VW was a good deal for five hundred dollars, but I perspired all the way to the office in the summer and froze all the way home in the winter. It shimmied so much it changed lanes on the freeway, even though I held the steering wheel straight.

I sought a professional opinion at a repair shop, and the mechanic later called and asked me to come down to talk with him. He refused to tell me over the phone what he had found, but he did say, "There is definitely something wrong with your front end." I feared the repair would cost more than the five hundred dollars I paid for the car. When I arrived at his shop, the mechanic lifted the carpet and exposed a large, rusty hole. He said,

"Reverend, you do not have any front end left. It is completely rusted away. The only thing holding your steering box is four sheet metal screws." I asked, "So, can I drive it for a couple of months?" He said, "Son, this car should not be driven ever again."

I learned firsthand that day that driving all over Houston in a car held together by four sheet metal screws was driving on divine time. Water is powerful, whether it threatens drowning or creates rust.

I once saw a sign that said, "History is not what it used to be." Many people would like to work at a single company for most of their lives, but that way of life has changed dramatically. The unemployment waters are rising and it's a strenuous swim. I heard an interview with AT&T's president recently, in which he said he thought he "might be the only one working at AT&T with two temps if things keep going the way they're going." In today's world, we find that there is less job security and less security in the relationships that we have. However, there is more security in knowing that our loving and caring God keeps watch over our waterlogged souls.

We must let go of unnecessary things in deep water. Grasping or holding onto anything impedes our ability to tread water. Heavy clothing or objects in pant pockets will weigh swimmers down, making drowning more likely. The Beatitudes tell us that Jesus' assurance helps us out of deep water.

Competitive swimmers get set on their diving boards or pool sides and wait for a whistle or horns to start the race. False starts happen when they dive before the horn sounds. Jesus cautions us about spiritual "false starts" when we dive before His signal. This caution is valuable because *"Heaven and earth will pass away, but my word will never pass away"* (Luke 21:33). God gives us time to follow His signal. His words assure us that He will be there even if we dive into the deep end of the pool. God controls the meek, and they will inherit the earth.

Luke 12:16-21 records the parable of the rich fool who decided he'd build bigger barns, but his soul was required of him that night. We should be careful because Luke 12: 23 says, *"Life is more than food, and the body more than clothes."* We need the right assurance policy when we are in deep waters.

The Needed Enlightenment

The eye is the lamp of the body. If your eyes are good, your whole body will be full of light. But if your eyes are bad, your whole body will be full of darkness. If then the light within you is darkness, how great is that darkness! No one can serve two masters. Either he will hate the one and love the other, or he will be devoted to the one and despise the other. You cannot serve both God and money. Matthew 6:22-24

Enlightenment is the second element that helps us make more sense of the blessed meek. Matthew records, *"The eye is the lamp of the body. So if the eye is sound your whole body will be full of light; but if your eye is not sound, your whole body will be full of darkness"* (Matthew 6:22-23). I believe different levels of darkness exist: at one level we can still see, at a second level the stars seem much brighter, and at a third level pervasive darkness prevents you from seeing your own hand held right before your very eyes.

We had a swimming pool when our children were young and we often took night swims. Turning off the lights and going under water was a great adventure. The darkness was like a blanket that increased the swimming risk, so we waited until our eyes adjusted to the ambient light.

Jonah swam in darkness when the sailors threw him overboard in the middle of a storm. The inside of the great fish had no lighting system and Jonah endured darkness for *"three days and nights"* (Jonah 1:11-17). Jonah prayed: *"You hurled me into the deep, into the very heart of the seas, and the currents swirled about me; all Your waves and breakers swept over me"* (Jonah 2:3 NIV). Jonah knew the deep, dark waters.

There is light in the deepest waters: *"Thy word is a lamp to my feet and a light to my path"* (Psalm 119:105). Jonah 2:1-2a reports, *"Then Jonah prayed to the Lord his God from the belly of the fish, saying, 'I called to the Lord out of my distress and He answered me.'"* God saved Jonah from the dark waters and the fish's belly: *"And the Lord spoke to the fish, and it vomited out Jonah on the dry land* (Jonah 2:10).

God answers prayers (Matthew 7:8) and pulls drowning swimmers from the dark waters. When I was president of LIFE Pacific College, a student asked me, "Do you know someone who has a car to give away?" We prayed. A few days later someone approached me and said, "I have a car to give away; in fact, we have two." We gave the cars to students and that led to other donors who gave ten cars to students and families that sought answers to prayer. Enlightenment is the second element of meekness.

Personal Burdens

Therefore I tell you, do not worry about your life, what you will eat or drink; or about your body, what you will wear. Is not life more important than food, and the body more important than clothes? Look at the birds of the air; they do not sow or reap or store away in barns, and yet your heavenly Father feeds them. Are you not much more valuable than they? Who of you by worrying can add a single hour to his life? And why do you worry about clothes? See how the lilies of the field grow. They do not labor or spin. Yet I tell you that not even Solomon in all his splendor was dressed like one of these. If that is how God clothes the grass of the field, which is here today and tomorrow is thrown into the fire, will He not much more clothe you, O you of little faith? So do not worry, saying, 'What shall we eat?' or 'What shall we drink?' or 'What shall we wear?' For the pagans run after all these things, and your heavenly Father knows that you need them. But seek first His kingdom and His rigorousness, and all these things will be given to you as well. Therefore do not worry about tomorrow, for tomorrow will worry about itself. Each day has enough trouble of its own. Matthew 6:25-34

The third element of meekness relates to our personal burdens—our stuff. Worrying about stuff can become the weight that pulls down the best of swimmers. My wife and I are candidates if there is a job available for worriers. Our ability to turn a fun-filled day into a worry-filled evening amazes us, but Jesus offers comforting words that leave little doubt about His meaning: *"So do not worry, saying, 'What shall we eat?' or 'What shall we drink?' or 'What shall we wear?' …Therefore do not worry about tomorrow, for tomorrow will worry about itself. Each day has enough trouble of its own"* (Matthew 6:31, 34).

Jesus encourages us not to worry about food, clothing, anxious thoughts, or our other stuff. The stuff we collect causes worry and may control our lives, but this experience is contrary to the Christian meekness that puts God in control. Since we have been given the gift of grace, what could possibly be left to worry about? D. A. Carson writes about how God's generosity counters worry:

> There are some famous examples of…such reasoning [about God's generosity] in the New Testament. Perhaps the best known is Romans 8:32: "He who did not spare his own Son, but gave him up for us all—how will he not also, along with him, graciously give us all things?" God has already given us His best gift; how much more will He give us lesser gifts? [51]

An Unassuming Swimming Style

Some people who live in negative situations may consider their experience normal. They may dog paddle for so long that they settle for far less than they could achieve with Jesus. The Israelites had been captives in Egypt's deep waters for generations and accepted their plight as normal. Although Israel did not ask for one, the writer of Judges reports that God raised up Samson as a deliverer. (See Judges 14-15.) The people of Israel had lived for so long under another's dominion that deep waters became a way of life. They asked Samson, *"Do you not know that the Philistines rule over us?"* (Judges 15:10). Worry and the burden of what we eat, drink, or wear, can become a heavy weight in deep water. Willard notes that God offers an alternative:

> Soberly, when our trust is in things that are absolutely beyond any risk or threat, and we have learned from good sources, including our own experience, that those things are there, anxiety is just groundless and pointless. It occurs only as a hangover of bad habits established when we were trusting things—like human approval and wealth—that were certain to let us down. Now our strategy should be one of resolute rejection of worry, while we concentrate on the future in hope and with prayer and on the past with thanksgiving. [52]

Christ, however, can teach us to swim efficiently when we keep our eyes on His goals and submit to His control. I believe that over ninety-percent of what we worry about never happens. God saved Noah from the flood and Jonah from the watery depths, and Jesus pulled Peter from the deep waters. Jesus challenges us as He challenged Martha when He said, *"Martha, Martha, you are worried about so many things"* (Luke 10:41). This verse remains a true proclamation to all who wrestle with the same life struggles. Personal burdens, our stuff, constitute the third aspect that keeps us in deep waters and threatens to drown us.

Virgie was in deep waters, close to death and about to give up. Her story perfectly captures this book's message about deep waters, the danger of drowning, and meekness in the recognition that God controls everything and reaches out to us with His strong hand. She was in her mid-seventies and surgeons had operated on her heart several times, but it was wearing out. She had constant pain and fainted at least once daily. She went to the hospital many times in ambulances she could not afford and knew the outcome would be the same—the physicians said nothing could be done.

Virgie dog paddled with all she had. She worried about money, her husband, the future, and dying. I spent many days with her and her husband and we prayed and talked. She said to me one day, "Pastor, tell me about heaven," so we searched the scriptures and formed a friendship by swimming together in her dark waters.

After Virgie fainted a few weeks later, the emergency responders found no pulse and she was rushed to the emergency room yet again. I came to the hospital just as they revived her through the third and last electrical cardioversion. She asked to see me, and said, "Pastor, I am not worried about the future any more. Only a few seconds ago, I was in a wonderful place and heading towards God. Every step I took, I got younger and younger. When I stood before him, I was as a young woman in my late teens. I could breathe easily, all my pain was gone, and I felt as if I were floating! Then suddenly, I was back in this body, on this table hurting from head to toe. I want you to know I grabbed the physician's coat and said these words, 'Don't you ever do that again!' I am not worried about dying anymore."

About four months later, Virgie made her final journey as she floated away freely without worries and filled with God's assurance. She relaxed in her struggles because she knew God was in control and she could swim toward His outstretched hands. Meekness produces a gentle, humble, considerate, and unassuming swimming style that trusts God.

God calls us to lead a blessed and meek life. The waters are deep and dark and we might drown, but God's kingdom is unshakable and He reaches toward us with His saving grace. The dog paddle technique doesn't work, but God's hands are strong and secure.

LESSON SEVEN:

Turning Your Boat Around

Blessed are those who mourn, for they will be comforted. Matthew 5:4

Explanation: Matthew 7:1-6

We were heading in our boat to a great fishing hole that had proven abundant at least a few times in the past. Anchoring our boat, we allowed the little guys—my son and daughter—to get their hooks in the water. About six hundred feet away, a boat began to go in circles right in the middle of the lake. My kids laughed as the boat continued its circular path, causing us to become dizzy just from watching. Laughing, pointing, and wondering what was going on in that boat, many others had gathered on the shore and in the water, watching as the drama unfolded.

It was about twenty minutes before a patrol boat edged its way toward the slow circling boat. After repeated loudspeaker announcements and attempts to get the driver—yes, there was someone behind the wheel—to stop the boat, which was a seemingly impossible task, the patrol boat followed in the same pattern until it was able to come along side. We had all speculated about the cause: health issues, heart attack, or worse. In the end, the boat's driver was out cold from too many beers. This experience allowed me a great time to talk to my children about drinking and for us to pray for him and his family. The man's boat was only able to head in one direction, but if he had been sober, he would have changed his direction in order to chart the right course for his planned destination. Instead, he found himself handcuffed and on his way to a jail cell, which was surely not what he had had in mind at the beginning of the day.

Repentance does not come easily to those who are trying to keep from drowning. It does not matter if you have a raft, a kayak, or a large boat—if you cannot change course to avoid dangers or obstacles ahead, a shipwreck is sure to happen. Repentance "signifies to change one's mind or purpose, always, in the New Testament, involving a change for the better, an amendment, and always, except in Luke 17:3-4, of repentance from sin." [53]

I have always heard that repentance meant to turn around, or go in a different direction. The seventh Beatitude (in our inverted order) will open up to us the greatest need of man towards God. We are to mourn, but we may ask, "To mourn over what?" Mourning will be overcome with rejoicing and comfort when the mourner understands what it means to become a "blessed mourner".

True repentance means turning our boat around in time so that our choices lead to the course corrections needed to find the comfort of God's forgiveness. The first course correction is to acknowledge that we are hopelessly lost and, in all certainty, going in circles. Calling out our own sin brings the comfort of knowing that dealing with our own sin first can save others in the same boat as us.

Again, when Jonah acknowledged his own sin first, the storm ceased and the rest of the passengers and crew on the boat were saved. God spared Jonah when he repented in the belly of the great fish and He then turned him back around and headed him towards home.

The Purpose of Mourning

Blessed are those who mourn, for they will be comforted. Matthew 5:4

At first reading, this Beatitude appears to offer more questions than answers. It seems to be more about our spiritual progression as we chart our course with Christ. There are times when running low on fuel in our boat, we can forge ahead or need to turn around and head back the way we came. Knowing when to turn around—and having the ability to do so—is what brings freedom and comfort.

There is a difference between how the world sees things and how God sees things. The world's Beatitudes would be more like, "Happy are the rich, for they are the ones who have all that matters; happy are the pushers, for they get what they really want; happy are the decision makers, for they control their own destiny; happy are those who always gripe, for they get their way in the end; happy are the non-committed, for they are never disappointed."

Now, consider a couple of the Beatitudes as written in the *Phillips Modern English* translation:

> *How happy are those who know their need for God, for the kingdom of heaven is theirs! How happy are those who know what sorrow means, for they will be given courage and comfort! Happy are those who claim nothing, for the whole earth belongs to them! Happy are those who are hungry and thirsty for true goodness, for they will be fully*

satisfied! Happy are the merciful, for they will have mercy shown to them! Happy are the utterly sincere, for they will see God. Matthew 5:3-8 [54]

We know that we walk under the scrutiny of God. We talk about His ideals, and we walk in His ways trying to grasp the reality that what happens here is not all there is. Cope, adjust, and do not worry that your boat is sinking—just keep on paddling.

Mourning reminds us that how we live is really about how much happiness we can experience by dealing with the sin *"that so easily entangles us"* (Hebrews 12:1). We are being taught to use our boating equipment so that we may prevent ourselves from crashing on the rocks while heading to port. The rudder that guides the boat is the central part to keep us on course, making the needed corrections.

In the same way, mourning is the rudder that keeps us on task, reminding the follower of Jesus that true comfort comes from knowing when to turn around and go in another direction.

Mourning

My understanding of mourning begins with our own lives, our own faults, and our own sins. Matthew 7:1-6 associates this Beatitude with looking at your own life before judging others; thus, I would restate this Beatitude as, "Blessed is the man that is moved to sorrow over his own sin."

Paul states, *"Godly sorrow brings repentance that leads to salvation and it leaves no regret"* (2 Corinthians 7:10). The book of Joel reminds us, *"Return to Me with all of your heart. Weep and mourn"* (Joel 2:2). Jesus relates again, *"I tell you, no! But unless you repent, you too will all perish"* (Luke 13:3). The book James reminds us, *"Grieve, mourn and wail. Change your laughter to mourning and your joy to gloom. Humble yourselves before the Lord, and He will lift you up"* (James 4:9). Jesus states again, *"I tell you the truth, you will weep and mourn while the world rejoices, you will grieve, but your grief will turn to joy"* (John 16:20).

Mourning plays a large part in a disciple's life. Here we are reminded to be careful of judging people above ourselves:

> This image and the sharp rebuke that follows suggest that what Jesus is concerned about is not the "imprudence" of judging other people but the presumption of condemning other people (who do bad things) as bad people and setting ourselves above them as their judges—as if we were not like them ourselves and never did bad things. [55]

We mourn over death, we mourn over sickness, we mourn over disobedience, and we mourn over defeat. God promises comfort when we mourn over our judgment of each other. When was the last time you were moved to tears, to mourning, over the world's sin? When did you hear something on the radio or the television, or read something on the internet that moved you so much that you mourned? Usually, we just get disgusted because we are so desensitized to what is happening in our world. When was the last time you wept over the brokenness of your own sin? How easy it is after following Jesus that we believe we just might be better than others.

I was drowning in my sin, and God spoke to me while I was selling bell-bottomed Levis at a clothing store, telling me that He would guide me on a path that would change my direction. I wept that day for my sin—my lack of understanding that God was real—and it changed my direction. This message from Matthew became more than ink and paper; it became a way to keep from sinking when the waters rose around me.

About two weeks later, something else took place. While sorting the pants, I looked around the store and wondered if any of these people knew that God was real? I looked around as tears filled my eyes, and I mourned for them. I was so deeply moved that I asked to leave for about an hour. I went to my car and cried from an overwhelming sorrow. Though I had little biblical knowledge, I experienced mourning for my own lost condition first, then for the lost around me. I judged my own life first, and found great comfort and, indeed, blessing from that experience of mourning.

This moment inspired my trips to Africa, to lead youth groups, and to pastor those people who God brought across my path. Weeping, accompanied by mourning, reminds us of the great cost of salvation—how we were first kept from drowning and how others still need to be pulled from the waters. Richard Foster notes:

> Our world is hungry for genuinely changed people. As Leo Tolstoy observes, "Everybody thinks of changing humanity and nobody thinks of changing himself." Let us be among those who believe that the inner transformation of our lives is a goal worthy of our best effort. [56]

God had so moved me during that time of my life that many of my friends came to acknowledge Christ as well. I knew who I was, and I was not impressed with my life before Christ. I knew God had forgiven me and I wanted to share His mercy with everyone. As promised, the comfort and blessing of God came after the mourning. It remains a dichotomy: Happy are you who cry—for you will find comfort.

Paul's Spiritual Progression

The way to God is the way of the broken heart. Paul's spiritual progression gives us a wonderful way to track his growth as he grew to understand the grace of God in keeping him afloat. Paul, the great Apostle, has written for us approximately one-third of the New Testament—Philippians, Colossians, Ephesians, and Romans have all been attributed to him. We are now able to take some of Paul's early and later letters and see how life reflections evolved, as he grew older following Christ.

Paul's first self-reference establishes his role as a leader of the church. He writes a letter against false teaching about the Spirit versus the Law. *"I, Paul, an apostle of Jesus Christ"* (Galatians 1:1). He is bold, confident, and commanding. In the ninth verse of chapter one, Paul continues his claim, *"As we have already said, so now I say again: If anybody is preaching to you a gospel other than what you accepted, let him be eternally condemned!"* We find little humility in these early writings; but at this time, conflict was inevitable, as the Law was becoming so infectious to the early church.

Paul later traveled to Athens where he preached the gospel with few results and many debates. He would eventually make his way to Corinth and find a new way to present the gospel. In the book of 1 Corinthians, Paul says, *"When I came to you brothers, I did not come with eloquence or superior wisdom as I proclaimed to you the testimony about God. For I resolved to know nothing while I was with you except Jesus Christ and Him crucified"* (1 Corinthians 2:1-2). Paul was not without contention and harsh criticism and he had a real impact on the Corinthian church, describing himself to them as *"the least of the apostles"* (1 Corinthians 15:9). With time comes more humility.

Paul's progression again surfaces in his writings after five or six more years of ministry. On one of his missionary journeys, Paul goes to Ephesus, where he experienced a fruitful ministry. In his decision to write a letter to the church in Ephesus, Paul proposes to lift up the glories of Christ. He states in the second chapter:

> *"Now to Him who is able to do immeasurably more than we ask or imagine, according to His power that is at work within us, to Him be glory in the church and in Christ Jesus throughout all generations, forever and ever! Amen."*
> Ephesians 3:20-21

Can you understand the breadth or length or height or depth of the love of God found in Christ Jesus our Lord?

Paul again defines his name and life in this letter, *"Although I am less than the least of all God's people"* (Ephesians 3:8). This progression comes with the revelation that God is always working on our hearts. Paul comes to the realization that his life is short. He has been brought to Rome and awaits his own death, yet while in prison he writes to Timothy—a young man in faith—to encourage him in his growth. The letter offers an understanding of his true position, *"Here is a trustworthy saying that deserves full acceptance: Christ Jesus came into this world to save sinners—of whom I am the worst"* (1 Timothy 1:15).

In the four letters Paul wrote, he reveals the downward mobility that leads to upward acceptance. We are all drowning. The waters are deep, but Jesus came to save us and in that we may find great comfort. Mourning starts with us first and then we can see more clearly to help others.

The Place of Judgment

Matthew's explanation in chapter 7:1-6, as associated with the seventh Beatitude, will place us directly in line with judgment. Glen H. Stassen speaks of judgment not as condemnation, but as forgiveness:

> Here as elsewhere, Jesus teaches a restorative justice that goes beyond what the Pharisees do in their fastidious practice of excluding whoever and whatever is impure. His teachings do not condemn nonconformist but instead restore outcasts to community. Far from imposing an authoritarian tradition on everyone who appears to be out of step with the authorities, this kind of justice encourages practices that produce mutual help in community. Helping others follow Jesus in their lives. [57]

The Proclamation

Matthew 7:1-6 has no room for exceptions; in it, we will find how judgmental we have become. There are four areas to consider about personal accountability—how we learn to navigate this world, so as not to find ourselves driving in circles.

The first is this proclamation, when Jesus tells us, *"Do not judge, or you too will be judged"* (Matthew 7:1). We could interpret this counsel as "don't rock the boat" and pursue peace at any price. However, in a few more verses, Jesus tells us, *"Don't give pearls to pigs"* (Matthew 7:6), encouraging us to be discerning about those around us.

Jesus is not proclaiming that we should never judge—but when we do, judgment comes back to us. Someone said to me once, "Judging is like throwing a cactus, it will hurt them, but it will hurt you, too." We must all make judgments in our lives and be ready to have judgment given back.

Westminster Catechism defines the church as "a place where God's word is preached, where sacraments are taken, and where discipline is given." Even early definitions of the church identified it as a place of discipline and correction. What would it be like if we never gave correction and never judged another person's motives?

While boating, there are rules that you will be judged by. You cannot swim outside of the designated areas. Children under the age of twelve must wear a life vest at all times while in the boat. You must travel counterclockwise on a lake to insure the safety of all boaters. When any of these boating laws are violated, you are judged. To tell another boater his or her faults—while you do not follow the rules yourself—leaves you open for the judgments that you have made.

A woman was caught in the very act of committing adultery. The teachers of the law and the Pharisees brought her to Jesus and declared: *"We have caught her and the law demands she be stoned."* They waited for the teacher to respond. Jesus said, *"Alright, go ahead. First one without sin, throw the first stone, I am with you."* The older ones walked away first, then on down to the youngest. Jesus tells the woman to leave and sin no more. Although judgment was deserved, what she received was forgiveness (John 8:1-11). She was drowning and Jesus gave her a hand into His lifeboat.

Mourning means starting with our own sins, then helping others.

The Practice

Do not judge or you too will be judged. For in the same way you judge others, you will be judged, and with the measure you use, it will be measured to you. Matthew 7:1-2

If we are not careful while judging, we may find that the act promotes a spirit of self-righteousness. Love is the central practice in judgment, as Paul states, *"It always protects, always trusts, always hopes, always perseveres. Love never fails"* (1 Corinthians 13:7-8). Instead, many times within the church we criticize all things, judge all things, and complain about all things. We seem to be waiting like sharks attracted to blood, circling in the water for the right moment to judge. What we measure out will be measured back to us.

There have been many times that we do not practice what we preach. In our communities, we should be more in tune with what is happening and what is changing around us. My ears become more attentive whenever I hear people say the words "they" or "them". Our practice must include the measure of criticism we give out and we must be willing to receive it. It begins with mourning over our faults—then we will be in the right place of humility to deal truthfully with what needs to be confronted. How many of "them" have been singled out as the reason for our community's issues?

If we use platitudes instead of practicing giving God His place, and engage in prejudice instead of principles, we stand guilty in our own judgment.

The Problem

Why do you look at the speck of sawdust in your brother's eye and pay no attention to the plank in your own eye? How can you say to your brother, "Let me take the speck out of your eye," when all the time there is a plank in your own eye? You hypocrite, first take the plank out of your own eye, and then you will see clearly to remove the speck from your brother's eye. Matthew 7:3-5

When it comes to sawdust and logs, we tend to get the two confused. If we are going to attempt to take a speck from another person's eyes, we must be able to see clearly by first removing what is lodged in our own eyes.

Mourning that brings comfort will start in our hearts and lives first. Jesus is not telling us to never try to clear another's vision. He simply wants to make sure we have cleared our own vision first as we see in Matthew 7:3 when He says, *"Why do you look at the speck of sawdust in your brother's eye and you pay no attention to the plank, or the beam in your own eye?"*

Many people have been to Israel and have gone swimming in the Dead Sea. Sinking in the Dead Sea is impossible because of the high salt and chemical compounds—and because of this, you will find out quickly that you should not splash any of that liquid into your eyes. I discovered this for myself one day when I was paddling around and a speck went right into my eye. It felt as if someone had thrown a handful of salt into my eye and I was blind! Though only a small amount, the seawater felt like a beam in my eye. From then on, I knew I would have much more empathy for the others swimmers who encountered the same thing in the Dead Sea.

When the beam is removed from my own eye, I am at a much better place to help others who cannot see. If you need an optometrist to have your eye looked at, do you go to a blind one? How can someone who is blind help somebody get a piece of sawdust out of his eye? Have you ever had a little piece of sawdust or a grain of sand in your eye and it felt much bigger than it actually was? We have all said to someone, "This thing is big, help me get it out," only to find out it was just an eyelash.

The problem that has grown and spread from generation to generation is what I call "beam disease". We have all been exposed, and now we all display the symptoms. This disease has formed different strains of problematic judgment. Lloyd-Jones speaks to us about dealing with our lives first:

> What a wonderful piece of logic this is! When a man has truly seen himself he never judges anybody else in the wrong way. All his time is taken up in condemning himself, in washing his hands and trying to purify himself. There is only one way of getting rid of the spirit of censoriousness and hypercriticism, and that is to judge and condemn yourself. It humbles us to the dust, and then it follows of necessity that, having thus got rid of the beam out of our own eyes, we shall be in a fit condition to help the other person, and to get out the little mote that is in his eye. [58]

We delude ourselves into thinking that we can judge in God's place. We judge whether someone is worthy; we judge how they look and where they work. Beam disease has now manifested itself in almost every area of our lives and we must find the cure, or we will bring judgment upon ourselves.

The problem remains that no matter the situation, we will all drown; the only safe harbor, calm waters, or seaworthy vessel is found in Christ. Repentance will cleanse the eyes through tears of mourning, which leads to the comfort of knowing the forgiveness of Christ. The first thing wiped away in heaven will be tears. When the eye has something in it that needs to be removed, our body's first response is tears. The best way to help another without false judgment is by walking with them through our own tears. The tears of a friend heal the heart and assure you of not being alone.

When you are swimming far from shore and need to find the right direction, another's loving tears will help turn you around and head you in the right path.

The Provision

Do not give dogs what is sacred; do not throw your pearls to pigs. If you do, they will trample them under their feet, and turn and tear you to pieces. Matthew 7:6

In this verse, we see that Jesus balances judgment with discernment and He tells us that judgment must start with ourselves first. Each of us who has received His forgiveness must ourselves be discerning, as discernment keeps us heading in the right direction. Jesus differentiated between the sheep and the goats. Paul made a discerning call by the Spirit of God to preach to the Gentiles, because the Jews, as he said, *"were tearing him to pieces."*

Willard addresses the need for discernment:

> Such easy misunderstandings as are now current make it all the more important that we be very clear in our minds what condemnation is and how it relates to the more basic sense of judgment that only involves "separating" one thing from another to the best of our ability. We simply cannot forsake discernment, and Jesus himself devotes the last half of Matthew 7 to urging us precisely to discern and, in that sense, to "judge". But we must forsake the practice of condemning people, and that will not be difficult at all once we see clearly what it is to condemn and have previously rid ourselves of anger and contempt. [59]

Discernment will keep us in constant relationship with Jesus; He knows how quickly waters that appear calm can become a storm within minutes. The warning of the Holy Spirit can save your life through discerning choices and through people helping us to change direction before the storm tries again to drown us.

The Plan of Forgiveness

You then, why do you judge your brother? Or why do you look down on your brother? For we will all stand before God's judgment seat. It is written: "As surely as I live, says the Lord," every knee will bow before me: every tongue will confess to God. Romans 14:10-11

The Beatitude offers blessing and comfort to the mourner who will deal with his own life first. The judgments we make, the beams we carry, and the need for true discernment lead us to strive for repentance. Without repentance, we are sinking in deep waters where there are no footholds. Forgiveness by God that is extended to others identifies the true Christian.

Recognize that others are simply different. Since I was twenty years old, I have traveled to East Africa and learned to live in a very different culture. In some African cultures, to be in a hurry is considered rude. It is customary to take your time, have some tea, and wait—never rush the conversation, for that would be rude.

Americans live in a multicultural country with many different ethnicities and values. People are different; to judge them without understanding the larger context is to devalue their worth. At the same time cheap grace is not what the world seeks, as Bonhoeffer addresses in his book *The Cost of Discipleship*:

> "But do we also realize that this cheap grace has turned back upon us like a boomerang? The price we are having to pay today in the shape of the collapse of the organized

Church is only the inevitable consequence of our policy of making grace available at a low cost." [60]

Mankind seeks truth that crosses culture and backgrounds. The gospel was preached to several groups—Samarians, Jews, and Greeks—each with their own issues and beliefs. Many times the gospel was rejected, for it seemed impossible to believe. Repentance was the baptism of John, and it required men to turn away from their sin and turn to God.

"Blessed are they that mourn" (Matthew 5:4) compels us to reflect upon our lives first. When you realize "I am going to drown," you face the fact that you need someone greater than yourself.

As I get older, I realize how in my youth I believed I could make it through anything. But the farther you get from shore and the more water you swallow, mortality begins rushing in. Repentance allows us to turn in another direction and forgiveness is the floatation device to get us there. Mourning over your life first brings clear eyes and a right heart, and then we are able to help guide and discern with those in such great need around us.

I have found that crying while swimming washes our tears away, leaving only the person next to us able to see them. The next time you mourn over the world, do not be surprised if it starts to rain, for God will be crying right next to us.

LESSON EIGHT:

Kingdom Swimming Lessons

Blessed are the poor in spirit, for theirs is the kingdom of heaven. Matthew 5:2

Explanation: Matthew 7:7-12

Although I was raised without a swimming pool, that did not stop me from learning how to swim. When I was eight, my family and I stayed in a hotel on vacation and we were all enjoying the water. I found a round life preserver—the kind of doughnut-shaped ring that might be used if someone was drowning. I somehow decided that using it as a floatation device would be fun—and, for a while that was true.

Like any child, I eventually became bored just holding on to it and had what I thought was a brilliant idea. I put the ring around my feet and floated around for a while. As I soon learned, this experience would be the complete opposite of fun. With the ring securely placed around my feet, I let go of the side of the pool and I was immediately flipped upside down with my feet above water and my head under. Where the adults were during this experiment, I am not sure, but it was only seconds before a family member got my head up and my feet out of the contraption. The life preserver—created to help save lives—in my hands had become a tool for sure drowning had I been by myself in the pool that day. Through this experience, I learned never to go swimming alone. We should always have a swimming partner to make sure that if things go wrong, someone else is there to help.

In the kingdom of heaven, the greatest swimming partner is assigned to *"never leave us, never forsake us"* (Hebrews 13:5). We can count on Jesus to keep us from drowning, as His teachings keep our heads above the water.

The Kingdom of Heaven

The Sermon on the Mount is one of the most pointed and passionate messages in the Bible. The sermon that Jesus spoke by the Sea of Galilee at Capernaum was a profound teaching. This young itinerant preacher, believed by some to be the Son of God, had come to save all men from drowning. The last Beatitude—poor in spirit—reminds us that those who can become poor and dependent only on God to save them will inherit the kingdom.

Though around water all my life, until recently, I had never had the resources or opportunity to go scuba diving. Just passing middle age, I went scuba diving for the first time when my wife and I traveled to Hawaii to celebrate our thirty-fourth wedding anniversary. What a gift my wife gave to me!

The first test that day was to swim in a confined area (a pool) to get the hang of the tanks and breathing. I quickly took to the equipment and was considered a natural swimmer. Afterwards, we joined a boat that would take us to lava caves for about a thirty-minute dive. I was excited, scared, and, as the oldest diver, hoped that I would not hold my partners back.

Going down about fifty feet—and looking up at the safety of your boat floating on top of the water—can be unnerving. Every breath I took was from the tank strapped to my back. I will have to admit there is nothing natural about it. Scuba divers are coached to breathe normally, but under the water, I was oxygen-poor, needing every breath to be provided through the tanks.

What a feeling it was when we headed back up to the top at a slow pace and were back on the boat! I had stared death in the face, yet swimming to the safety of the boat without incident was a victory! Once you breathe on your own, you forget that you were so poor that you could only trust the oxygen in your tanks to support your life.

For every breath—in every part of life—we are totally dependent on God. As we are reminded in Matthew 6, *"What shall we eat…what shall we drink…your Father knows that you need them…seek first the Kingdom of God."* (See Matthew 6:25-34.) The poor in spirit are those who know they are dependent only on God.

I remember a radio advertisement some thirty years ago that said, "Man can live forty days without food, three days without water, and one second without hope." That is the truth for the poor in spirit—we must rely every moment on God to fill our spirits. Phillip Yancey admits there is but one way to live this ideal:

> "There is only one way for any of us to resolve the tension between the high ideals of the gospel and the grim reality of ourselves: to accept that we will never measure up, but that we do not have to. We are judged by the righteousness of the Christ who lives within, not our own." [61]

Children of the Father

Jesus speaks a lot about God as our Father throughout the Sermon on the Mount. In the time of Jesus, to claim that God was your Father would have been considered blasphemous. Jesus' declaration, *"My Father is always at his work to this very day, and I too, am working"* (John 5:17) was an invitation for a stoning. Jesus came speaking and daring to proclaim that we are all the children of God.

The Sermon on the Mount mentions the Father's relationship to man eight times, being very specific in most of its applications. Jesus said, *"Then your Father who sees what is done in secret, will reward you"* (Matthew 6:4). Adding as well when we pray, *"This then, is how you should pray: Our Father in heaven..."* (Matthew 6:9). Jesus gave us much to think about with the statement, *"Be perfect as your heavenly Father is perfect"* (Matthew 5:48).

We are reminded that only one repays when Jesus states, *"But when you pray, go into your room, close the door and pray to your Father, who is unseen"* (Matthew 6:6). Again while fasting, we are to seek this truth, *"When you fast, put oil on your head and wash your face, so that it will not be obvious to men that you are fasting, but only to your Father who is unseen"* (Matthew 6:17-18).

Toward the end of the sermon, Jesus commands that our relationship with the Father include our "stuff" when He says, *"So do not worry, saying, 'What shall we eat?' or 'What shall we drink?' or 'What shall we wear?' For the pagans run after all these things, and your heavenly Father knows that you need them"* (Matthew 6:31-32).

Jesus disseminated this message about our relationship to the heavenly Father. In this emphasis, Jesus relates that the gospel has far-reaching effects in its scope and power. It must bring us to the realization that we cannot swim long enough to keep from drowning.

While growing up, we were unable to go into the deep end of the pool if we were not able to swim across safely without dog paddling, and once that was accomplished, the whole pool was ours! The kingdom of heaven is just like that pool. We are limited in access and without hope if we cannot swim in the kingdom correctly. The Beatitudes are the lessons that teach how to get to the other side.

Once we understand this principle—that we are poor and unable to accomplish this effort on our own—the blessings of the Beatitudes and the entire kingdom of heaven is ours!

Poor in Spirit, not Poverty of Soul

Being poor in spirit and having poverty of the soul are two different things. This idea of being poor in spirit is one of the greatest promises of the New Testament. With uncertain futures, living in an unstable world, and facing job cuts, we can see here the uncompromising pledge of this biblical message.

The Alpha and Omega—beginning and end—teaches the crowds, while thousands of years later we read His words, the promise of *"Ask and it will be given you"* (Matthew 7:7). Though imbalance abounds in a "name it and claim it" theology, Jesus has already in chapter six of Matthew assured us that His Father knows what we need. We are not to worry about the present or the future, for when we ask, there is someone listening and ready to answer. There is nothing more irritating for me than being on hold for an hour, wondering when a live person will respond to my question. Though we know answers from the Lord may be "yes" as well as "no"—and sometimes even "wait"—we are assured that we are being heard.

Eugene Peterson reminds us that asking and prayer must be a way of life:

> Prayer must not be fabricated of our emotional fragments
> or professional duties. Uninstructed and untrained, our
> phrase book: we give thanks at meals, repent of grosser
> sins, bless the Rotary picnic, and ask for occasional

guidance. Did we think prayer was merely a specialized and incidental language to get by on during those moments when we happened to pass through a few miles of religious country? But our entire lives are involved. [62]

How many of us have sought something we really wanted—a position, a relationship—only to find out years later what a blessing it was that it didn't happen? There will be times when we need to be reminded that God hears us and knows what is best for us.

It is important to note that there is a difference between having poverty of the soul and being poor in spirit. Poverty of the soul can be described as having given up internally—when inside has become a wasteland of loss with no hope of change. While serving the church as a pastor, I have come across people who have developed a poverty mentality. This experience is not associated with any prosperity imbalance; these are merely people who have learned to live spiritually at a level where God would say to them, "I have more for you." Poverty of the soul feels like there is no way out and that your only option is to adjust and accept your fate. Poverty of soul is like losing the drain plug from your boat while you are trying to bail out the water. It will continue to rush in even as you do your best to get rid of the water.

In contrast, those who are poor in spirit will realize they need another's help. You will not remain where you are if you are "asking, seeking, and knocking". We are to be poor in our spirit, but not impoverished in our souls

We must come to recognize that the basis of the Sermon on the Mount is that we are broken, drowning, and far from safety. Jesus has come to lift us from the deep waters and place us where He can watch us—just as He did with His disciples! I am convinced that the reason Jesus walked on the water was that it was the only place people could not get to Him! But, it was more likely that as the disciples were driven from shore and were in fear of drowning, Jesus walked to them. Crying out, He heard them, and came to rescue them from the storm.

The poor in spirit cry out often—seeking answers quickly and banging on closed doors. Being poor in spirit may not only be about our physical situation, although Jesus certainly addresses that condition in the sermon. I believe it is also about how our spiritual lives are in daily need of His help. We cannot live on yesterday's prayers or past insights and understanding. We need a fresh relationship with God this day, this hour, this moment. We need Him to keep us from drowning, and to help us live out His teachings so that our salt and light is most effective. Asking, seeking, knocking, will keep us swimming and heading in the right direction.

John Ortberg will remind us that in order to walk on water, you have to get out of the boat. He says,

> But the Lord is passing by! Jesus is still looking for people who will get out of the boat. I don't know what this means for you. If you get out of your boat—whatever your boat happens to be—you will have problems. There is a storm out there, and your faith will not be perfect. Risk always holds the possibility of failure. But if you get out, I believe two things will happen. The first is that when you fail—and you will fail sometimes—Jesus will be there to pick you up. You will not fail alone. You will find that He is still wholly adequate to save. And the other thing is, every once in a while you will walk on water. [63]

In response to a woman who anointed Jesus with oil and myrrh, Jesus said to His disciples, *"The poor you will always have with you"* (Mark 14:7). Although this mixture was very expensive and used for burial to anoint the body, the woman anointed Jesus with this very costly mixture to the ridicule of those who had gathered around. Jesus did not agree and reminded them that what she did will always be remembered. It was not about money, but about obedience.

The poor in spirit are constantly asking and seeking the heart of God, for they will inherit the kingdom of heaven. The poor will always be here and we are to reach out to them in order to make a difference. That the poor must ask and seek becomes a lesson for our spiritual lives.

Three things seem to manifest when we pass from poor in spirit to a hopeless soul of spiritual poverty. One of the first things I noticed was that I was learning to settle for less. For instance, I decided one recent summer that I was going to learn how to wakeboard. Now, I had been waterskiing for years, but this experience was completely different. I did not want to ask for help and had determined I could do this myself. The entire summer was filled with different water events with me being pulled behind the boat and diving like a submarine, coming up gasping for air. Finally a friend—who was an avid wakeboarder—watched and gave some simple instructions, which I heeded. On the next few attempts, I was up on top of the water! That is where you have the most fun and the greatest freedom. All those times I was being dragged under water, I was attached to my stubbornness and impoverished view of the situation. I just knew there was no way I could do this. I thought I was too old to be learning how to wakeboard. I had exhausted all of my ideas to make it work and still was having no success. However, the peace and fulfillment I finally felt that day was worth the wait.

How many times have we exhausted ourselves and, due to a deprived outlook, stopped asking, stopped praying? We settle for less and do not pursue getting up on top of whatever situation we face. Those who are spiritually impoverished seem to attract those who will allow them to settle for less.

The second manifestation I noticed is that there are people who are spiritually impoverished, who cannot receive what God wants to give them. They seem to develop spiritual hearing loss toward His Word and

His promises. Hope has diminished and they adjust their hearts to give up on receiving anything from the Lord.

Paul was heading to Rome by way of Crete when a dangerous storm arose. He had seen in a vision that they would be saved, but the ship would be a total loss. In the midst of the storm, many of the men began to fear for their lives and sought to escape in the lifeboats, believing that the large ship would hit the rocks. Paul reminded them, *"Unless these men stay with the ship, you cannot be saved. So the soldiers cut the ropes that held the lifeboat and let it fall away"* (Acts 27:31).

There will be times in our own lives where we must become dependent on God alone. "Lifeboats" we use today can be things like past relationships, old habits, or things we hold on to just in case we cannot stay the course. God will ask each of us to cut away things we think will help in times of trouble. The only help that Paul could give to those men was listening to the Word of the Lord. And, the only way we will fully inherit the kingdom of heaven is to be poor in spirit.

Lastly, I saw that poverty of soul finds people functioning in the spirit of a widow, which can be defined as one who gives off the sense that the best has gone—the things that I longed for have already been taken from me and cannot be replaced. I would appeal that we should be more like a bride than a widow. The best is yet to come, and we can still dream of the future.

While the poor in spirit will inherit the kingdom of heaven, the soul of poverty is swimming against the current, always falling behind. In other words, Jesus is saying, "Happy is the person when you are poor in spirit, for that is a state of being." It does not say, "Blessed in spirit are the poor."

Myron Augsburger speaks to us about the value of asking, seeking, and knocking:

> The threefold command to ask, seek, and knock is both command and invitation. These words are present

imperatives in the Greek, which mean continues action. Ask and keep asking. This may suggest persistent effort, but more likely it is the recognition that we need to continually come to God. We should not think that, having asked once, we are presumptuous to ask again. In fact the progression suggested in the words "ask", "seek", "knock" may suggest growing awareness of our dependence on God. [64]

When you are poor, you have to ask and there is reliance upon others. People will stand on street corners holding signs that declare, "I need food." Christians should be declaring before God, "My spirit is poor, God, I need you today." The poor in spirit ask God for help, seek Him for relationship, and knock continually until He opens the door.

Being poor in spirit does not mean you go around with sadness, stating in effect, "Yes, I'm poor in my spirit." Blessed are you when you realize that only God can build the spirit. When we realize our inadequacies, our destitution, and our inability to fill one moment with anything of value, we understand the magnitude of the kingdom of heaven.

The greatest swimming lesson is never to swim alone! The lessons that are learned in seeking and asking make us dependent on God for our very lives. Paul writes in 2 Corinthians, *"For you know the grace of our Lord Jesus Christ. That though He was rich, yet, for your sakes He became poor, that through His poverty, you might become rich"* (2 Corinthians 8:9). Whenever we pray, we are asking, seeking, and knocking for God's presence.

Swimming on Your Knees: Asking, Seeking, Knocking

Ask and it shall be given you; seek and you will find; knock and the door will be opened to you. For everyone who asks receives; he who knocks finds; and to him who knocks, the door will be opened. Matthew 7:7-8

Bill McKenzie had been a tugboat captain in the Port of Houston all of his life. I was a young youth pastor and Bill wanted to buy me a suit, so we went to a department store where he decided he was going to buy one as well. While trying on our suits, the salesman was helping and hovering around us. Bill came out with the pants on and loudly made his wants known. His voice, reminding me of a fog horn, declared for all in the store to hear, "These pants are too tight, I have to able to get on me knees. I have worn out two pairs of suit pants being on my knees praying."

I know that you can pray standing up, but no matter to Bill—those pants he bought had to give! Bill taught me that day that prayer was the most important thing we do. I have never forgotten this.

While some people have such fear of the water and swimming, lessons can help them adjust and assist them in losing the fear of drowning. Prayer to the disciple is what the life vest is to the fearful swimmer. One of the things learned while taking swimming lessons is that your body is made up mostly of water, which will indeed help keep you afloat. Kingdom swimming lessons reveal that prayer will keep you above the water and heading towards God, no matter the strength of the current that is coming against you.

Lessons of Prayer

Ask and it shall be given you... Matthew 7:7

Asking is the first lesson of prayer that I have often called "whatever prayer". Paul says to, *"Pray without ceasing"* (1 Thessalonians 5:17). God is never to be excluded from any situation in our lives. We read in the book of Joshua, *"The men of Israel sampled their provisions but did not inquire of the Lord"* (Joshua 9:14). That mistake of not inquiring of the Lord cost Israel for years to come.

"Whatever prayer" is to become a way of life, always bringing before the Lord our needs no matter how important or unimportant we may deem them. We always need to ask for His involvement. Some of the biggest problems in my life have happened when I did not bother to ask for His help.

...seek and you will find... Matthew 7:7

The second lesson of prayer is seeking God. Seeking is prayer wherever you may find a need. As Psalm 139:7-10 says:

> *Where can I go from Your Spirit? Where can I flee from Your presence? If I go to the heavens, You are there; if I make my bed in the depths You are there. If I rise on the wings of the dawn, if I settle on the far side of the sea, even there Your hand will guide me, Your right hand will hold me fast.*

Where can we go from God's presence? Elijah found God even in the storm that raged outside his cave. Finding God should take on the same essence as breathing. It is second nature—but find yourself choking and you realize how important breathing really is. Prayer is no different. Remember the kingdom of heaven is given to those asking whatever and seeking wherever.

...knock and the door will be opened to you. Matthew 7:7

The third lesson of prayer is that we are to keep on knocking—we are to be in prayer about all things at all times. Oftentimes, we may think that we have to put off praying until it seems "more appropriate". However, prayer is always the right thing to do, and "whenever" is the right time.

Israel's day would begin at night, as was the order of creation. The Sabbath begins at sundown and ends the next night about mid-evening. I have often awakened in the morning thinking that the day is now beginning. But, God has reminded me that my day is already half over, and

I should be asking Him what He has been doing while I have been sleeping. The day does not start when we wake up, but when we pray!

The three aspects of the poor in spirit have us asking, seeking, and knocking whenever, whatever, and wherever we have need of God's help.

In his exposition of Matthew, the author agrees:

> The first Beatitude has already set the tone: God's approval rests on the person who is poor in spirit. Such a person, recognizing his personal spiritual bankruptcy and his personal inability to conform to kingdom perspectives, will be eager to ask God for grace and help, impatient to seek blessings only God can give, delighted to knock at the portals of heaven. He also recognizes that salvation now—and the full richness of that salvation in the consummated kingdom—depends on God's grace, God's free unmerited favor. This man rejoices to read Jesus' invitation to ask, seek, and knock. He comes as a humble petitioner, seeking pardon and grace. [65]

The Rich Reward of Heaven

Which of you, if his son asks for bread, will give him a stone? Or if he asks for a fish, will give him a snake? If you, then, though you are evil, know how to give good gifts to your children, how much more will your Father in heaven give good gifts to those who ask Him! So in everything, do to others what you would have them do to you, for this sums up the Law and Prophets. Matthew 7:9-12

The book of Isaiah says, *"Before they call, I will answer. While they are still speaking I will hear"* (Isaiah 65:24). It seems that we speak much about prayer and find the act of prayer impossible to sustain.

Being poor in spirit reminds us that we need God's presence in all that we call life. Jesus concludes this section in Matthew with the compassion of an earthly father and the promise of our Father in heaven. If the Kingdom can come by asking, then by all means ask! The great privilege we have been given is to come without fear and believe that our Father listens and will give good gifts to His children.

My daughter swam the longest heats for her college team—grueling one thousand yard heats where pacing is everything. Such exertion is not for the fast sprinters, but for those who have worked up longer stamina. I have thought—even after swimming two pool lengths—that there must be some kind of insanity in wanting to swim all those laps. My daughter swam an average of three miles a day. This endurance did not come immediately; there were many weeks of training, working on her breathing, and developing her strength.

Prayer is not something you can be proficient at immediately. The poor in spirit are those who see the long goal ahead. We are not in this to finish first, but to finish well. Learning the techniques of asking, seeking, and knocking assures the swimming disciple that the lessons will pay off. The rich reward of heaven is promised to those who acknowledge that those around us need to be treated as we would like to be.

Remember—there are those who are splashing wildly around us, fearful of drowning, just as we once were. Treat them as we have been treated, and together we will find calm waters and shelter in stormy times.

THE FINAL LESSON:

A Titanic Conclusion

In 1912, the great passenger liner *Titanic* set course for New York City, determined to break the existing record for the fastest crossing of the Atlantic Ocean. She was three football fields in length, and included a full-size swimming pool, gymnasium, and a darkroom to develop pictures.

One *Titanic* crewmember was heard to have stated, "Even God himself could not sink this ship." The ship was traveling at full steam, somewhere around twenty-four miles an hour. Though she could carry over 3500 passengers and crew, there were only twenty lifeboats. Although she was designed to carry forty-six lifeboats, they cluttered the walkways, so the extras were removed from the ship. The *Titanic* was designed to withstand four compartments to be breached and still stay afloat—but the iceberg they hit damaged five—and mere feet kept the ship from staying on top of the water.

In Genesis, the earth's flood rose above the highest mountain by twenty feet; the men, women, and children of the *Titanic* were only a few miles from having been rescued. After sending distress signals by telegraph and even shooting off rockets, the *Titanic* sunk within two hours of being damaged.

Though it was the mechanical wonder of the age, the ship's crew neglected to have even one lifeboat drill. From the captain down to the last crewmember, none felt a drill necessary, for they believed that the boat was unsinkable. If they had slowed down...if they had paid more attention... if they had listened to the earlier telegraph messages of icebergs...they might never have lost over fifteen hundred lives that fateful morning. The crew was unwilling to listen to what they had been told and they failed to practice even the rudimentary exercise of having lifeboat drills that might have saved twice as many lives.[66]

The Sermon on the Mount's conclusion should compel all who have read this teaching of Jesus to begin to put into practice its very words. As the *Titanic* ignored the most basic of exercises—lifeboat drills—we should not neglect putting into practice these lifesaving lessons.

There is great scholarship that would exclude the teaching of Jesus as symbolic; others would seek the application as more relevant during great persecution, in view of Christ's return. I find it very difficult when Jesus states in Matthew, *"Therefore everyone who hears these words of mine and puts them into practice"* (Matthew 7:24), to dismiss them as great ideals that we cannot emulate. Bonhoeffer states,

> "It is evident that the only appropriate conduct of men before God is the doing of His will. The Sermon on the Mount is there for the purpose of being done (Matthew

7:24 ff.). Only in doing can there be submission to the will of God." [67]

Perfection is the daily action of choosing to live like Christ by putting His teachings into practical application as a lifestyle. We will never be finished, but pressing on to become all that God has for us is part of being a disciple.

The Sermon on the Mount is not inclusive of every area needed for growth and wholeness, but must be taken and practiced as a part of the whole counsel of God. For me, the Beatitudes and the explanation found in the sermon has been a lifesaving teaching that I have practiced for the past thirty years. We may never reach a place of maturity that fully satisfies us, but until Jesus returns, this message reminds us of our daily need of Him.

The True Entrance

Enter through the narrow gate. For wide is the gate and broad is the road that leads to destruction, and many enter through it. But small is the gate and narrow the road that leads to life, and only a few find it. Matthew 7:14

When we choose to follow the Lord, the gate is narrow at its inception and the road continues to shrink. The road to life is a rather narrow way and few choose that path. The wide road, however, is inviting and offers the acceptable means of being like everyone else. That road, if unchecked, leads to the deep waters of no return and no hope.

Once you accept that Jesus has called you to follow Him, your way will appear like an ocean, very wide and easy to transverse. When I first came to Christ, I felt I was on "easy seas", as my life at first did not change much—I was in waters that were neither rough nor demanding.

After some months, a few storm clouds appeared and a new current directed my life towards a certain course. Over the past years, my river has continued to narrow until it has become a creek! No longer needing to question everything, I have become better at swimming as well. I have heard that many people drown in water that is not even over their heads. There is something psychologically challenging about being in deep water, especially when you cannot see the bottom—but you can drown in three feet of water just the same.

The key is knowing that no matter how deep the waters are, or how rough the storm has become, when you have been swimming with nothing left but the fear of drowning, Jesus will come to you—either walking on the water or guiding His boat over to you—with the assurance of safety.

The True Tests

When you own a pool or spa, you must test the water on a weekly basis, measuring the chlorine and keeping the pH (acidity) in balance. You cannot see the difference at first, but if left unchecked, the water will become cloudy and very soon unhealthy for swimmers. These tests are essential to keeping swimmers safe.

The concluding thoughts of the Sermon on the Mount are three tests that will keep the swimmer safe and the waters pure from false prophets, fake fruit, and phony people:

> *Watch out for false prophets. They come to you in sheep's clothing but inwardly they are ferocious wolves. By their fruit you will recognize them.* Matthew 7:15-16

A false prophet is one that, especially in the Old Testament, comes before people with false judgments, speaking divisively and appearing sincere, although with very subversive motives.

There are also false prophets among us today just as there have been throughout all the history of Israel. These are people who speak falsely in the name of Christianity, bringing division to the body of Christ. False doctrine, false living, and false commitment will lead many to follow a false message. Just as Paul reminded the Galatians not to be fooled by any other gospel that would falsely add to the free gift of salvation, we must be attentive as well:

> *Every tree that does not bear good fruit is cut down and thrown into the fire. Thus, by their fruit you will recognize them.* Matthew 7:19-20

There are false prophets who will come—and then there is fake fruit. In my home as a child, we had several platters of fake fruit, which looked real enough until you got up close. In the 1970s, decorative green grapes and wax apples were plentiful in homes across America. Fake fruit cannot be eaten, have little value, and collect dust!

Although the fake fruit that my mother had in our home lasted until we threw it away, the fake fruit that Jesus is referring to does not last. Study someone long enough and if they are false, it will be revealed. The fruit they produce will be easy to spot and will allow you to understand that bad fruit comes from rotten trees.

Fake fruit and false prophets have not found the narrow road that leads to life; they follow the wide road and make their own way. The application of this teaching will separate the false from the true and the fake from the real:

> *Not everyone who says to me "Lord, Lord," will enter the kingdom of heaven, but only he who does the will of my Father who is in heaven.* Matthew 7:21

The final accusation comes from Jesus about people who are not who they pretend to. Phony people are those who speak religious words, and even act accordingly, but have not surrendered themselves to fulfill God's will. They may even come to church, live next door, and seem like good people.

Mankind has always tried to add or subtract from what is built only by grace. The waters rose twenty feet above the highest mountain, and all drowned except those in the ark. People can try to explain, argue, and even show their good works, but there is only one way to the kingdom of heaven. We cannot simply act right, give to worthy causes, or even use the right language—the outcome remains the same.

Works will not save us and new swimsuits will not keep us from drowning. The entire message comes from the lessons that will get us to safety. I will not be able to talk my way into heaven, fake my way into heaven, or even prophesy my way in. I will enter heaven because Jesus knows my name and will make sure that He is with me. I cannot keep these blessed Beatitudes on my own, but with his grace, I will become like him, applying them to my daily living.

Moses complained to God that he had nothing to come to Pharaoh with to make him change his mind. God heard him and said, *"Throw your staff down."* When he did, it immediately became a serpent and when he picked it up it turned back into his staff. Moses might have said, "Cool, I can do something with this." He went to the pharaoh and said, "God says, 'Let my people go,' and look what I can do!" He threw the staff down—I am sure with great delight—but the pharaoh did not seem at all bothered that he had snakes in his house. Instead, he ordered his priests to throw their staffs down and they all became snakes. What was the difference, since they performed and had the exact same results as Moses? It was that Moses' snake ate all the other snakes—a little trick that God failed to tell Moses about—which revealed the real from the phony. (See Exodus 7.)

The truth of our relationship with God is based on our name. Though God did not have need of a name, we are clearly known by ours. Relationships are built on trust, respect, and knowing each other's name.

My wife and I dated for four years before we were married. If I always referred to her as "what's-her-name", our relationship would have lacked in personal growth, to say the least. Likewise, our relationship with God must be intimate enough that He knows us by name and we respond when He calls.

During jury duty a few years ago, a man was asked how often he spoke to his son, who was a police officer. His response was amazing: "I speak to him about once a year." His response grieved me because of what it must have represented about their relationship. I speak with my son, who is married with three kids, almost every day. I cannot conceive of anything else.

Many times I think that people speak to God once a year, and assume the relationship is all it needs to be. *"I never knew you"* (Matthew 7:23) must be one of the most haunting and convicting of statements. Those are the words no one wants to hear from any family member—and certainly not from God.

The Guarantee

Therefore everyone who hears these words of mine and puts them into practice is like a wise man who built his house on the rock. The rain came down, the streams rose, and the winds blew and beat against that house; yet it did not fall, because it had its foundation on the rock. But everyone who hears these words of mine and does not put them into practice is like a foolish man who built his house on sand. The rain came down, the streams rose, and the winds blew and beat against that house, and it fell with a great crash. Matthew 7:24-27

Jesus concludes the Sermon on the Mount with this unbelievable caveat: When you buy a new boat, the waters you float above could at any time put the safety of friends and family at risk. You must make sure that there is a warranty or a guarantee. We should ask the usual questions, such as "what is covered?" and "how long does it last?" A new boat comes with extended guarantees that create trust in the product, but if we put these Beatitudes into practice, is there a guarantee?

The concluding remarks are the most impressive of guarantees. The very nature of water reminds us that we could drown in shallow coves and calm seas. "How can I keep from drowning?" requires the same answer as the jailer who asked, "How can I be saved?" in Acts chapter 16. Paul's response, *"Believe in the Lord Jesus Christ and you will be saved"* (Acts 16:31), is the correct response.

In the book of Matthew, Jesus concludes, *"Therefore, whoever hears these words of mine and puts them into practice is like a wise man who builds his house on a rock"* (Matthew 7:24). When the storms rock your boat, and the winds of adversity blow against you as you swim, the guarantee is that the rock can be trusted. Build on it and you will not be disappointed. Hearing and doing are coupled to the promise that the rock will withstand whatever we face. To hear, and yet not try putting these Beatitudes into practice, makes you a very foolish individual. Your house cannot stand without the application. The promise of future security is a house built on the rock, which gives the boater, swimmer, and dog paddler the hope that even though the waters are twenty feet above the highest rock, Jesus will pass by to rescue all who are practicing in faith the lessons that will save them from any potential threat or uncertain storm.

The crowds were amazed at Jesus' teaching. He spoke with such calm and conviction that they remarked at His authority. Read again these words, and study anew this pivotal and powerful sermon, which was a declaration of hope and practice. Blessed are those who swim with Jesus right by their side or who have Him right there in the boat with them. These lessons have kept me from drowning more than once. Though all of Scripture is for correction, reproof, and growth, something about these three chapters in Matthew have changed my drowning life.

Yancey has this concluding insight:

> For years I had felt so unworthy before the absolute ideals of the Sermon on the Mount that I had missed in it any notion of grace. Once I understood the dual message, however, I went back and found that the message of grace gusts through the entire speech. It begins with the

Beatitudes—Blessed are the poor in spirit, those who mourn, the meek; blessed are the desperate—and it moves toward the Lord's Prayer; "Forgive us our debts…deliver us from the evil one." Jesus began this great sermon with gentle words for those in need and continued on with a prayer that has formed a model for all twelve-step groups. "One day at a time," say the alcoholics in AA; "Give us this day our daily bread," say the Christians. Grace is for the desperate, the needy, the broken, those who cannot make it on their own. Grace is for all of us. [68]

"*Therefore everyone who hears these words of mine and puts them into practice…*" Matthew 7:24. Concluding with this verse, I have but one word: Amen!

Notes

[1] Yancy, Philip. (1995). *The Jesus I Never Knew* (134-135). Grand Rapids, MI: Zondervan.

[2] Stassen, Glen H. (2006). *Living The Sermon On The Mount* (39). San Francisco, CA: Jossey-Bass.

[3] Stassen, Glen H. and Gushee, David P. (2003). *Kingdom Ethics* (46). Downers Grove, IL: InterVarsity Press.

[4] Lloyd-Jones, David Martyn. (1960). *Studies in the Sermon on the Mount* (133). Grand Rapids, MI: William B. Eerdmans.

[5] Kinnaman, David. (2007). *Un Christian* (131). Grand Rapids, MI: Baker.

[6] Willard, Dallas. (1998). *The Divine Conspiracy* (127). San Francisco, CA: HarperCollins.

[7] Wells, Ronald A. (1989). *History Through the Eyes of Faith* (238-239). San Francisco, CA: Harper.

[8] Bonhoeffer, Deitrich. (1963). *The Cost of Discipleship* (126). Originally translated from German by Neville Norton Smith 1949. New York, NY: Macmillan & Co.

[9] Kenner, Craig S. (1997). *Matthew* (114). Downers Grove, IL: InterVarsity.

[10] Carson, D.A. (1987). *Jesus' Sermon on the Mount* (44). Grand Rapids, MI: Baker Books.

[11] Willard, Dallas. (2009). *Knowing Christ Today* (180). New York, NY: HarperCollins Publishers.

[12] Stassen, Glen H. and Gushee, David P. (2003). *Kingdom Ethics: Following Jesus in Contemporary Context* (45). Downers Grove, IL: IVP Academic.

[13] Augsburger, Myron S. (1982). *Mastering the New Testament* (64). Dallas, TX: Word.

[14] Strong, James (1990). *The Strong's Exhaustive Concordance of the Bible* (930). Nashville, TN: Thomas Nelson.

[15] Willard, Dallas (2006). *The Great Omission* (100). New York, NY: HarperCollins Publishers.

[16] Keener, Craig (2009). *The Gospel of Matthew: A Socio-Rhetorical Commentary* (100). Grand Rapids, MI: Wm. B. Eerdmans Publishing Co.

[17] Peterson, Eugene H. (1992). *Under the Unpredictable Plant* (22). Grand Rapids, MI: Wm. B. Eerdmans Publishing Co.

[18] Bonhoeffer, Dietrich (1995). *The Cost of Discipleship* (152). New York, NY: Touchstone Books.

[19] Willard, Dallas (2006). *The Great Omission* (100). New York, NY: HarperCollins Publishers.

[20] Lloyd-Jones, David Martyn (1984). *Studies in the Sermon on the Mount* (32). Grand Rapids, MI: Wm. B. Eerdmans Publishing Co.

[21] Willard, Dallas (2009). *The Divine Conspiracy* (117-18). New York, NY: HarperCollins Publishers.

[22] Stassen, Glen H. and Gushee, David P. (2003). *Kingdom Ethics: Following Jesus in Contemporary Context* (45). Downers Grove, IL: IVP Academic.

[23] Wierzbicka, Anna (2001). *What did Jesus Mean? Explaining the Sermon on the Mount and the Parables in Simple and Universal Human Concepts* (104-05). Oxford, England: Oxford University Press.

[24] Vine, W.E. (1940). *Vine's Expository Dictionary of New Testament Words* (60). Tempe, AZ: The Bible Foundation BBS.

[25] Lloyd-Jones, David Martyn (1984). *Studies in the Sermon on the Mount* (318). Grand Rapids, MI: Wm. B. Eerdmans Publishing Co.

[26] Jordan, Clarence (1972). *The Substance of Faith and Other Cotton Patch Sermons* (69). New York, NY: Association. Quoted from Stassen and Gushee, Kingdom Ethics (138).

[27] Carson, D.A. (1987). *Jesus' Sermon on the Mount* (52). Grand Rapids, MI: Baker Books.

[28] Stassen, Glen H. and Gushee, David P. (2003). *Kingdom Ethics: Following Jesus in Contemporary Context* (92). Downers Grove, IL: IVP Academic.

[29] Keener, Craig (2009). *The Gospel of Matthew: A Socio-Rhetorical Commentary* (128). Grand Rapids, MI: Wm. B. Eerdmans Publishing Co.

[30] Willard, Dallas (2009). *The Divine Conspiracy* (177). New York, NY: HarperCollins Publishers.

[31] Stassen, Glen H. and Gushee, David P. (2003). Kingdom Ethics: *Following Jesus in Contemporary Context* (140). Downers Grove, IL: IVP Academic.

[32] Piper, John (1979). *Love Your Enemies* (1). Cambridge, MA: Cambridge University Press. Quoted from Wierzbicka, What Did Jesus Mean? (111).

[33] Carson, D.A. (1987). *Jesus' Sermon on the Mount* (56). Grand Rapids, MI: Baker Books.

[34] Vine, W.E. (1940). *Vine's Expository Dictionary of New Testament Words* (174). Tempe, AZ: The Bible Foundation BBS.

[35] Lloyd-Jones, David Martyn (1984). *Studies in the Sermon on the Mount* (312). Grand Rapids, MI: Wm. B. Eerdmans Publishing Co.

[36] Hybels, Bill (2002). *Courageous Leadership* (22). Grand Rapids, MI: Zondervan.

[37] Bonhoeffer, Dietrich (1995). *The Cost of Discipleship* (47). New York, NY: Touchstone Books.

[38] Kenner, Craig S. (1997). *Matthew* (135). Downers Grove, IL: InterVarsity.

[39] Nouwen, Henri H. (1989). *In the Name of Jesus* (54-55). New York, NY: Crossroad.

[40] McLaren, Brian D. (2001). *A New Kind of Christian* (150). San Francisco, CA: Jossey-Bass.

[41] Lloyd-Jones, D. Martyn (1960). *Studies in the Sermon on the Mount* (18-19). Grand Rapids, MI: William B. Eerdmans.

[42] Peterson, Eugene H. (1987). *Working the Angles* (43). Grand Rapids, MI: Wm. B. Eerdmans.

[43] Willimon, William H. and Hauerwas, Stanley (1996). *Lord, Teach Us: The Lord's Prayer & the Christian Life* (20-21). Nashville, TN: Abingdon Press

[44] Willard, Dallas (2006). *The Great Omission* (195). New York, NY: HarperCollins Publishers.

[45] McGrath, Alister (1999). *Christian Spirituality: An Introduction* (3). Malden, MA: Wiley-Blackwell.

[46] Arndt, William F. and Gingrich, F. Wilbur (1963). *A Greek-English Lexicon* (705). Chicago, IL: University of Chicago.

[47] Vine, W.E. (1940). *Vine's Expository Dictionary of New Testament Words* (401). Tempe, AZ: The Bible Foundation BBS.

[48] Hagner, Donald (1993). *World Biblical Commentary* (92-93). Nashville, TN: Thomas Nelson. Quoted in Stassen and Gushee, Kingdom Ethics: Following Jesus in Contemporary Context (40).

[49] Lloyd-Jones, David Martyn (1984). *Studies in the Sermon on the Mount* (64). Grand Rapids, MI: Wm. B. Eerdmans Publishing Co.

[50] Tozer, A. W. (1993) *The Pursuit of God* (105). Camp Hill, PA; Christian Publications.

[51] Carson, D.A. (1987). *Jesus' Sermon on the Mount* (92). Grand Rapids, MI: Baker Books.

[52] Willard, Dallas (2006). *The Great Omission* (212). New York, NY: HarperCollins Publishers.

[53] Vine, W.E. (1940). *Vine's Expository Dictionary of New Testament Words* (401). Tempe, AZ: The Bible Foundation BBS.

[54] Phillips, J.B. (1952). *The New Testament in Modern English* (25). New York, NY: Macmillan & Co.

[55] Wierzbicka, Anna (2001). *What did Jesus Mean? Explaining the Sermon on the Mount and the Parables in Simple and Universal Human Concepts* (181). Oxford, England: Oxford University Press.

[56] Meade, Frank S. (1965). *Encyclopedia of Religious Quotations* (44). Grand Rapids, MI: Fleming H. Revell Co. Quoted in Foster, Celebration of Discipline (11).

[57] Stassen, Glen H. (2006). *Living The Sermon On The Mount* (144). San Francisco, CA: Jossey-Bass.

[58] Lloyd-Jones, David Martyn (1984). *Studies in the Sermon on the Mount* (181). Grand Rapids, MI: Wm. B. Eerdmans Publishing Co.

[59] Willard, Dallas (2009). *The Divine Conspiracy* (224). New York, NY: HarperCollins Publishers.

[60] Bonhoeffer, Dietrich (1995). *The Cost of Discipleship* (54). New York, NY: Touchstone Books.

[61] Yancy, Philip. (1995). *The Jesus I Never Knew* (142). Grand Rapids, MI: Zondervan.

[62] Peterson, Eugene H. (1987). *Working the Angles* (58). Grand Rapids, MI: Wm. B. Eerdmans.

[63] Ortberg, John (2001). *If You Want to Walk on Water, You've Got to Get Out of the Boat* (28). Grand Rapids, MI: Zondervan.

[64] Augsburger, Myron S. (1982). *Mastering the New Testament* (98). Dallas, TX: Word.

[65] Carson, D.A. (1987). *Jesus' Sermon on the Mount* (118). Grand Rapids, MI: Baker Books.

[66] Saballa, Casey (1994). *Titanic Warning* (27-84). Green Forest, AR: New Leaf Publishing Group.

[67] Bonhoeffer, Dietrich (1955). *Ethics, Volume 1955, Part 1* (43). Originally translated from German by Neville Norton Smith 1949. New York, NY: Macmillan & Co.

[68] Yancy, Philip. (1995). *The Jesus I Never Knew* (143). Grand Rapids, MI: Zondervan.

[69] Ramey, William (1996-2004). *Chiamus: Introduction*. Retrieved from http://www.inthebeginning.org/chiasmus/

Appendix A

Chiasmus Structure

Whereas many literary structures have been recognized in the Bible in the past (step parallelism, inclusion, etc.), a significant literary structure of biblical texts has received noted recognition in the past century, an especially in the past two decades, is CHIASMUS. Chiasmus, also spelled sometimes as "chiasm", is derived from a Greek verb meaning "mark with two lines crossing like as 'X'" (chi, the 22nd letter of the Greek alphabet). In general, chiasmus refers to an inverted parallelism or sequence of words or ideas in a phrase or clause, sentence, paragraph, chapter, or an entire literary work. For example, Matthew 7:6 contains a simple chiasmus that may be represented as follows:

> A "Do not give what is holy to dogs,
>> B and do not throw your pearls before swine,
>> B^1 lest they trample them under feet,
> A^1 and turn and tear you to pieces."

In this instance, the propositions A and B are reflected as in a reversed mirror image by the propositions B^1 (said as "B prime") and A^1 (said as "A prime"). By recognizing Matthew 7:6 as a chiastic structure, one can make much better sense of this verse than might otherwise be done; for it seems most logical that the dogs (A) tear to pieces (A^1), and the swine (B) do the trampling (B^1). Chiasmus involves fundamentally two elements: Inversion and Balance (as shown in the example above). These two main elements of chiasmus, inversion and balance, produce a third, climactic centrality. Looking at the above illustration, strictly speaking, it represents inverted parallelism rather than chiasmus. Thus, the uniqueness of the chiastic structure lies in its focus upon a pivotal theme, about which the other propositions of the literary unit are developed, whereby the author may compare, contrast, or complete each of the flanking elements in the chiastic structure. [69]

In the past fifty years, much has been written about order, sequence, letters, and numerology. I have read and studied many books over the past 30 years and have found many chiastic structures in the Old and New Testaments. Though I would agree that to use this form of study without balance could lead down a slippery slope of forced ideas and poor exegesis. However, within the ancient texts are found poems and prose—and in the Psalms, acrostics using the letters of the Hebrew language to begin each verse. So there is much to be read, studied, and adapted to experience the richness of the Word of God.

I have discovered in reading dissertations on the Sermon on the Mount from other colleges, they are varied in approach, yet many have developed similar ideas. (Fuller Seminary has a few exceptional projects.) Using the eight beatitudes in an inverted order, forming the outline for the Sermon on the Mount, is unique to this book. There may be others that have written or published the same premise, but I have not found them through my research and study materials.

I do not believe that the chiasmus that is found in this book to be the only way to study and preach the Sermon on the Mount. There has been a multitude of books written and study materials available on this sermon preached by Jesus. I have books that have been written covering only the eight beatitudes, as well as others who only give passing reference to the beatitudes and focus on the sermon in Matthew 5-7, as they write or create study materials.

Following the sequence of *"You have heard that it was said"* in the sermon, there seems to follow a natural break in the subject matter. Though it does not hold true for each of the eight beatitudes and their subsequent explanations, it does give an easy way to attach the beatitudes as a natural outline as shown in this book.

Further study on Chiasmus can be found in the following books:

Clarke, Thomas B. (2008). *Joshua's Spiritual Warfare: Understanding the Chiasms of Joshua.* Syracuse, NY: Prayer Gardeners.

Lund, Nils W. (1992). *Chiasmus in the New Testament.* Peabody, MA: Hendrickson.

About The Author

D r. Dan Stewart is the former President of Life Pacific College in San Dimas, California. He has served as a pastor in four different churches, and was the Director of LEAD, a training and equipping program for pastors within the Foursquare Church. In 1988, Dan joined Life Pacific College's faculty and has also taught at three other universities.

For over 35 years, he has traveled to East Africa to train, teach, and raise up leaders in the Mt. Kenya area. Dan enjoys mentoring and raising up younger leaders to engage this world and continues to teach, write, and lead yearly teams to Africa and Israel.

Dan and his wife, Connie, have three awesome children and live in Southern California.